BACK TO SCHOOL

BACK TO SCHOOL

Jewish Day School in the Lives of Adult Jews

Alex Pomson and Randal F. Schnoor

With a Foreword by Jack Wertheimer

WAYNE STATE UNIVERSITY PRESS

DETROIT

12 11 10 09 08   5 4 3 2 1

♾ The paper used in this publication meets the minimum requirements of the American National Standard for Information Sciences—Permanence of Paper for Printed Library Materials, ANSI Z39.48–1984.

Library of Congress Cataloging-in-Publication Data

Pomson, Alex.
Back to school : Jewish day school in the lives of adult Jews / Alex Pomson and Randal F. Schnoor ; with a foreword by Jack Wertheimer.
   p. cm.
Includes bibliographical references and index.
ISBN-13: 978-0-8143-3383-9 (pbk. : alk. paper)
ISBN-10: 0-8143-3383-4 (pbk. : alk. paper)
1. Jewish day schools—United States. 2. Jewish day schools—Canada.
3. Jews—United States—Identity. 4. Jews—Canada—Identity. I. Schnoor, Randal F.   II. Title.
LC741.P66 2008
371.076—dc22

                                        2007044691

Grateful acknowledgment is made to the Morris and Emma Schaver Publication Fund for Jewish Studies for the generous support of the publication of this volume.

Designed and typeset by BookComp, Inc.
Composed in Trump Mediaeval

June 12, 2008

Contents

Foreword

Jewish life in North America has been transformed in recent decades by massive shifts in outlook and behavior. Where once it was possible to identify a set of common assumptions among most Jews about the nature of their religious and ethnic identities, it has become increasingly difficult to build consensus about what it means to be Jewish. Some social observers, in fact, argue that self-constructed identities are the norm in our time and that identity is chosen freely by the "sovereign self" rather than shaped by communities of faith, ethnic groups, or other social entities. This change in outlook, in turn, both reflects and drives profound social changes, most notably increasing mobility. Jews are on the move, relocating to other regions or else to locations at an ever further remove from centers of Jewish settlement. Moreover, boundaries have collapsed between Jews and their neighbors, leading to unprecedented levels of social integration and intermarriage.

The result in behavior has been contradictory. While many Jews are gravitating away from involvement with any kind of Jewish collective, another group, albeit a smaller one, is spinning back into the orbit of Jewish collective activity, partially in reaction to unfettered freedom and opportunity and in search of a larger meaning for their lives. Indeed, the latter group has self-consciously and deliberately opted to heighten its participation in Jewish life, seeking out more and better Jewish education, intimate Jewish religious communities, and frequent opportunities to express Jewish connection through volunteering and philanthropic giving and creative expression using music, art, salonlike conversations, and the new media. Depending on which sector of the Jewish community one examines, it is "the best of times" or "the worst of times."

The bipolar movement of Jews toward and away from engagement has prompted reflection within the leadership of Jewish institutions, and in the 1990s produced a so-called continuity campaign to involve more Jews. Central to this effort was a new emphasis on Jewish education as the primary means to ensure continuity—and to rebuild commitment in Jewish life.

Over the past two decades, Jewish education has attracted greater attention and also philanthropic support. Enrollments in Jewish day schools rose significantly in sectors of the Jewish community that in the past had not been partial to this form of Jewish education, especially within the ranks of Conservative Jews. New thinking and programming has gone into the upgrading of supplementary Jewish schools. Summer camping has attracted new funding on the assumption that the intense experience of so-called 24/7 Jewish living can have a formative impact on impressionable young Jews. And other types of informal Jewish education, such as youth activities and trips to Israel, have also expanded. All of this effort has been given a further boost by a new body of suggestive research literature pointing to a strong correlation between multiple and sustained exposures to various types of Jewish education in childhood and adolescence on the one hand, and positive engagement with Jewish life in adulthood on the other.

Even with the energy that has been expended on improving Jewish education for young people, the field of adult education has undergone a renaissance. Two guiding assumptions undergird new experiments in Jewish adult education. First, if children are to be socialized successfully as active participants in Jewish religious and communal life, their parents must be enlisted as allies in the process, for parents can and ought to be the primary Jewish educators of their children. Certainly, they are the most important influences in shaping the identities of young people. Second, Jewish education will benefit if it is not seen as a solely pediatric exercise but rather as a lifelong process. The richness of Jewish civilization cannot possibly be communicated in a few years of childhood schooling and is so richly textured that Jews of all ages will find meaning if they are socialized to continue to educate themselves.

These two concepts in turn have guided the expansion of family and adult education. Several programs have now been created to engage adults in sustained multiyear programs of part-time study following graded curricula that move adults to deeper knowledge.

Other initiatives seek to ratchet up levels of Hebraic literacy and synagogue skills among the adult population. And still others specifically address adults in their role as educators of children, offering them guidance about how to be a Jewish parent.

Although much of this new effort originates in the work and promotion of educators and communal leaders—that is, it works from the top down—experiments in Jewish adult education have also been driven by changing interests and expectations within the adult population itself—that is, from the bottom up. If adults did not hunger for learning opportunities, such programs could not have gained a significant following. In the current climate, parents of school-age children behave as consumers and are not bashful about what they seek. Educators have begun to realize that parents choose to enroll their children in a school not only for what it will offer their children but also for the benefits it provides to parents in a setting that broadens their own Jewish knowledge and as a place to join a network of peers who share common interests. Parents now expect schools to not only engage their children but also engage them. In brief, Jewish schools increasingly are no longer only for children.

Back to School is a study of how a day school can serve as a source of meaning in the lives of adult Jews. In this groundbreaking study, Alex Pomson and Randal Schnoor investigate how parents choose schools and develop a theory to explain the school choices of families. The authors argue forcefully that parents are driven almost as much by the desire to find a place for themselves as they are by a concern to find the best fit for their children. Anyone interested in how Jewish educational decisions are made by families and how to address the explicit and implicit concerns of parents as they shop for a school will benefit from this rich discussion.

The book also contributes to our understanding of what the authors call "the school as shul"—that is, how the school assumes functions that "previously had been performed for adults by the synagogue." The particular day school under consideration, a non-denominational school in downtown Toronto, creates occasions that hold special meaning for parents, even as it serves as a setting for adult learning and a place of meeting for parents. The authors strengthen their case by demonstrating through comparative work outside of Toronto that other day schools of varying stripes and in entirely different locales also assume these new functions, even if not always by design. The needs of today's Jewish adults are propelling schools to assume new roles to help parents.

To further bring together the school with family life, the authors track the impact of "the school at home." They ask, "What meaning do families make of new information and approaches their children have absorbed in school? And how do families incorporate such learning into the existing culture of the home?" This in turn opens a still broader set of questions about the ways in which adults in the current fluid environment construct their identities through a series of new types of interventions and experiences. The authors argue that as fewer Jewish adults are exposed to Jewish learning during their own formative years, they must find alternative avenues to deepen their self-understanding and inform themselves about the breadth of Jewish civilization. Their children's schooling offers an unparalled setting for such exploration. Here, then, is a further example of how the authors go well beyond the school experience to draw broader conclusions about the construction of Jewish identity in our times.

Written in an engaging and accessible style, *Back to School* gracefully moves from the particular case of one closely studied school to a range of other day schools and then to matters of theory and generalization. As the authors correctly note, their study "sits at the intersection of the fields of education and the sociology of contemporary Jewry." Among the great strengths of this book is its authors' self-conscious reflection on their own research approach and their acknowledgment of its limitations. As the entire field of Jewish education goes "back to school" to rethink the basics, we would all do well to learn from this perceptive and charming book.

JACK WERTHEIMER

Acknowledgments

This was supposed to be a book about teachers, but it has ended up as one about parents. Parents, we have come to learn, constitute the great unexplored frontier for Jewish day-school education.

Such a profound reorientation of interests bears witness to a fruitful and always enjoyable collaboration between two people who brought together two different sets of concerns and created something new from their combination. One of the authors is a scholar of Jewish education, the other a sociologist of Jewish identity. We wrestled many times with the conceptual frame of the work. Is it a study in education? Is it an inquiry into Jewish identity? In the end we hope it contributes to both areas, while situated broadly in the sociology of contemporary Jewish life.

The reorientation of our inquiry not only reflects a productive long-distance collaboration but also is testament to the many ways in which we have benefited from the guidance and encouragement of colleagues. Foremost among these have been our colleagues at York University in the Centre for Jewish Studies and the Faculty of Education. At York, we owe a special debt of gratitude to Michael Brown and Marty Lockshin for their mentorship and friendship.

Colleagues at Hebrew University's Melton Centre for Jewish Education have always been generous with their wisdom and support. We are particularly grateful to Michael Rosenak and Howie Deitcher for their interventions at strategic moments in the development of this project.

Many chapters were first presentations at the annual meetings of the Network for Research in Jewish Education. The sympathetic but critical responses of colleagues in this forum have served as the furnace in which our ideas have been forged. Among our Network colleagues, Carol Ingall, Joe Reimer, and Michael Zeldin had a special influence on the work that has emerged here.

This project would not have been possible without the financial support provided by the Social Sciences and Humanities Research Council of Canada. In addition, data from "Centreville," discussed in chapter 6, were collected with funding provided by the AVI CHAI Foundation. Chapter 2 was written thanks to financial assistance provided by the Research Unit of the education department of the Jewish Agency for Israel.

Kathryn Wildfong, our editor at Wayne State, merits special thanks for her interest and encouragement from the first time we met and then over subsequent months. Jack Wertheimer, too, has been an example and guide in this project and others. We are flattered by his readiness to contribute a foreword to this volume.

Finally, we owe special thanks to a number of people at the heart of the study. We are profoundly grateful to the parents, teachers, and children at the Paul Penna Downtown Jewish Day School for welcoming us into their midst over a four-year period. We owe special thanks to Elysa Cohen, Michaele-Sue Goldblatt, and Janet Nish-Lapidus for facilitating our entry into the school, and then for allowing us to stick around even at difficult moments. We thank the parents of six other day schools who agreed to be interviewed as a comparative sample. The work that emerged benefited greatly from the wisdom and goodwill of Dafna Ross, who served as research assistant for the project over a two-year period.

Acharon aharon haviv, last but not least, Alex Pomson would like to thank his wife, Tanya, for her extraordinary dedication to his work and their family. Her support has been greater than any reasonable person could expect. As for Anna, Ori, Ittai, and Shifra, it has always been a joy to see their puzzlement at how Daddy could spend so long working on the same book. Randal Schnoor would like to thank his wife, Marsha, for her continual support of his work. She put up with countless evenings alone with their newborn daughter as her husband spent time "at the school" and in the homes of school parents. He will keep the lessons of this work in mind as he chooses a Jewish day school for Jaeli and her new brother, Shea.

Introduction

WHY STUDY DAY-SCHOOL PARENTS?

A Different View of Parents and Schools

There is something unsettling about the frequent bipolar depiction of the relationship between parents and schools. More often than not, the two parties are portrayed as "adversaries or advocates," as "partners or protagonists," or as "enemies or allies" (Crozier 2000; Cutler 2000; Webb and Vulliamy 1993). These multiple dichotomies bespeak an assumption of difference—of parents and schools as "worlds apart," in Sara Lawrence-Lightfoot's phrase. The two worlds might be bridged, but without great effort, it seems that they will dangerously collide (Lawrence-Lightfoot 1978). What brings these worlds into overlapping orbit is, of course, children. Children provide the occasion and site for their interaction.

Given the source of their connection, it is not surprising that the relationship between parents and schools has been of interest to researchers and policy makers almost entirely in terms of the consequences for children, or, to be precise, insofar as the presence or absence of parents shapes the quality of children's education. While over the last ten years there has been a proliferation of research literature that explores mothering and parenthood as forms of adult identity, few attempts have been made to connect these states with research on schooling (DiQuinzio 1999; Lewis 1999). Instead, it is as if two assumptions dominate when it comes to parents and schools: first, that most parents have already spent many years in school and are unlikely to find their adult associations with their children's schools to possess any special importance for their own lives; second, that the role of children's education in the life of the

1

family possesses little significance in comparison to the role of the family in children's education.

Although in recent years there has been increasing recognition that schools not only function to prepare children for life within particular religious, social, or occupational communities but also may influence the lives of parents, this recognition tends to focus on what may or may not ultimately benefit children. Thus, in the United States, with the emergence of charter schools, magnet schools, and school vouchers as educational options for millions of parents, there has been a modest move toward a more dialectical appreciation of the relationship between parents and their children's schools (Driscoll 1995; Smrekar 1996). In England, too, with the enactment of legislation establishing new roles for parents as consumers choosing schools and as governors managing schools, there has been a new interest expressed in making sense of the ways parents relate to their children's schools (Hughes, Wikely, and Nash 1994; Munn 1993). Yet such inquiries have not freed themselves from a paradigm that assumes a more or less unidirectional sequence of cause and effect in the relationship between parents and schools. This paradigm (one that can be traced back to the Coleman Report of 1966, which found that the home environment was of much greater influence on student learning than school-level effects such as organization, resources, and governance) minimizes the consequences of parent involvement in schools in terms of its meaning and significance for parents themselves (Gamoran, Secada, and Marrett 2000).

The gap that separates the study of Jewish schooling from the study of adult Jewish lives may be even wider than that in the disciplinary paradigm just described. While there is a venerable (and hotly contested) tradition of sociological inquiry into the impact of different modes of Jewish schooling on adult Jews, the intent of such research has been to consider the impact of Jewish education experienced during one period of time on Jewish identification expressed during another (Barack Fishman 1995; Cohen 1995; Lipset 1994). Usually retrospective in orientation, this research can be likened to a forensic scientist's attempt to reconstruct an event long past from the scars on a corpse. Similarly, while there is no less a substantial body of ethnographic and anthropological work that explores the place of various institutions, such as synagogues, charities, community agencies, and families, in the lives of Jewish adults (Furman 1987; Kugelmass 1986; Myerhoff 1979; Prell 1989), the notion that schools may play a significant role for the Jewish adults whose children they educate has been rarely considered, certainly not in the context of a book-length study. The few exceptions to this pattern have been either preliminary or limited in scope (Beck 2002; Kaplowitz 2002; Wall 1995), with the richest examples to be found in Reimer's (1997) study of life at a congregational school and Kovács and Vajda's (2002) examination of intermarried families at a Jewish day school in Hungary.

Typically, when researchers have crafted ethnographies of Jewish school life, parents have been viewed as contextual factors that make up the backdrop to the real business of school by making a once-and-for-all decision about whether a child should attend day school, supplementary school, or any Jewish school, in fact, and by coloring children's attitude to their Jewish education through displays of apathy or interest (Bullivant 1983; Heilman 1984). To put it bluntly, it seems to be assumed that parents went to school once before and therefore have little reason to return other than to fulfill carpool commitments, put in an appearance at parent-teacher meetings, or help schools raise money.

In the pages that follow we explore what may seem counterintuitive in light of the tendencies described earlier: we investigate the possibility that Jewish schools are important institutions in the lives of Jewish parents. Of course, we understand that schools are constituted first and foremost to educate and socialize children. As John Dewey famously put it, schools are places where society places all it has accomplished at the disposal of its *future* members (1902/1990). But this burden of educational responsibility does not preclude the possibility that schools also perform significant roles in the lives of *today's* adult members of society. Moreover, against the backdrop of sociological research in contemporary Jewry that suggests that there have been significant changes in the patterns of institutional engagement and involvement among Jewish adults, we explore the possibility that Jewish day schools may occupy a position of greater significance in the lives of some adult Jews than once seemed imaginable.

Inspirations and Assumptions

An inquiry such as this, which sits at the intersection of the fields of education and the sociology of contemporary Jewry, has a number of inspirations. In empirical terms, it grows out of what, for one of the authors, began as an attempt to develop a theoretically grounded study of the extent to which Jewish schooling realizes a genuinely alternative vision of education from that provided by the public school system. At a time when close to a quarter of a million children in North America are being educated in a school system that previously attracted a tiny minority of children from the Jewish community, Pomson intended to produce "a thick ethnography of a private Jewish day school at a contested moment in the history of public education in North America" (quoted from research proposal). He hoped that "the study [would] contribute to public discourse about the purposes and practices of private denominational education and [would] advance understanding of why parents choose such schools for their children." To that end, he approached DJDS, a small and recently established Jewish day school, to see if the school might serve as a field site within which to examine these concerns.

By the end of a five-month pilot phase (conducted during that time by Pomson alone), it became apparent that a significant part of the data related to the presence of parents in classrooms, corridors, and committees. It seemed that almost every time he visited the school he witnessed an episode or event in which parents were active and, on occasion, the only participants. Although he had worked for a number of years in Jewish high schools, he was unprepared for the intensity of such involvement. In the spirit of a grounded theory orientation to qualitative research, he was led by the data's composition toward considering why parents were so much of a presence in their children's school. He wondered what was happening to them as a consequence of their involvement and whether, on some level, they were attracted to the school and active in its life as much because of what it offered them as adults as because of what it promised their children (Pomson 2004). These interests prompted a grant application to the Social Science and Humanities Research Council to study if

and how Jewish schools serve as arenas for adult Jewish involvement and to examine how parents' Jewish identities shape and are
shaped by their relationship with their children's schools. This
successful application made it possible for Schnoor and Dafna
Ross (a doctoral candidate) to join the research team so as to
extend the number of research sites investigated and to develop
multiple research approaches that could pay attention not only to
the words and actions of parents but also to the perspectives of
teachers, administrators, and children.

Although these are the circumstances that launched this
inquiry, its theoretical inspirations came from a number of direc-
tions. Most narrowly, the notion of studying the relationships
between parents and their children's schools was inspired by a rich
tradition of research into the lives and experiences of teachers,
that other group of adults whose existence is tied up with schools.
Since the 1930s, sociologists of teaching have shown that schools
can mark, in sometimes brutal ways, the identities and values of
those for whom they serve as workplaces and whose daily lives are
conducted in their classrooms, corridors, and offices. Teachers, it
has been shown, although charged with effecting change in children's cognitive understanding and their developing characters,
are often no less changed by their time in schools than those
whose lives they are charged with changing (Acker 1999; Lortie
1975; Waller 1935/1960).

In speculating whether similar effects might occur for parents
as a consequence of their direct or indirect relationships with
their children's schools, this inquiry was informed in the most
general fashion by a poststructural view of culture and identity as
neither unified nor fixed but as always under construction. From
this perspective, school culture is not a singular entity (Sarason
1996) that reproduces (McLaren 1986) or challenges (Sergiovanni
2000) the social and political relations of the surrounding society.
It is more helpfully conceived as an "interface of individual and
collective responses to the problem of how best to educate the
child" (Henry 1993) and, in this instance, of how best to be both
Jewish and North American.

This inquiry was predicated, then, on a view of identity as constantly being made, unmade, and remade (Danielewicz 2001) in

response to and as a direct result of the "dialectical interplay of processes of internal and external definition" (Jenkins 1996). This does not mean that selves do not exist or are unrecognizable but, rather, as Stuart Hall (1997) has suggested, that they are apprehended in the positions people adopt (or are forced to adopt) at different times and places. People's performances are what make them (momentarily) who they are.

From this perspective it is reasonable to assume that parents are influenced by their involvements in their children's schools and that they may be influenced by their children's schools no less than they influence those schools themselves. If, as poststructural theorists suggest, our performances not only express who we are but also change us, then how we involve ourselves in our children's education (at home and at school, in parent committees, in meetings with teachers, and when talking about school with our children) will have some influence on our selves.

A last, and decisive, inspiration for the study and its particular interest in making sense of the significance for parents of their relationships with their children's Jewish schools came from the increasingly commonplace notion within the sociology of religion that people lead rich religious lives beyond the institutions once assumed to mark out the territory of an engaged religious life (D. Hall 1997; Orsi 1999). This last notion emphasizes what David Hall calls "lived religion"—how people understand and live out their identities as members of a religious community on an everyday basis, how they create the sacred and construct meaning in often spontaneous, frequently innovative and entirely personal fashion (Davidman 2003, 261). We wondered whether Jewish day schools might provide for parents an arena of "living religion" where they come to create their own alternative Jewish communities beyond the institutions that have historically framed Jewish life. In simple terms, we speculated whether for some Jews the school may rival the "shul" as the key locus of their personal Jewish engagement.

One of the earliest accounts of the restructuring of religious life from public to personal spheres was provided by Berger (1967), who proposed that although in the modern context religion continues to possess force in society, it exercises this influence in gradually smaller, and increasingly privatized, realms. What Berger called "the sacred canopy" of religion no longer provides an overarching frame of meaning for society as a whole. Instead, religion has been reduced to narrower spheres, namely personal and family life (Roof 2003).

Empirical support for Berger's "privatization" thesis has come from a variety of contexts and faith traditions. In the United Kingdom it was provided by Davie (1994), who, in reflecting on the coexistence of low levels of church attendance in Britain with evidence of persisting widespread belief in God, developed a concept of what she called "believing without belonging." She argued that ours is not so much an age without faith as one where traditional conceptions of sacred places, and organizational memberships in general, have diminished appeal. Religious identity neither calls for nor depends on association with a particular place of worship; it is more individualistic, inward looking, and privatized. Wuthnow (1998) referred to this same trend as a shift from a "spirituality of dwelling" to a "spirituality of seeking."

Following extensive research in numerous aspects of civic life in the United States, Putnam (2000) proposed a radical expansion of the privatization thesis. He showed in the most compelling fashion that the turn inward from corporatism and collectivism that had been widely observed among mainline churches was less a consequence of changing expressions of religious belief and more the result of broader developments in civic life since the 1960s. A generalized decline in face-to-face engagement—in what one might call belonging *with* or *without* believing—had afflicted national charities, political parties, and even bowling leagues, and it derived from a generalized erosion in social capital (day-to-day, face-to-face interactions between adults) as people turned to their families and to elements in their private lives to find satisfaction and meaning.

The fullest examination of such trends among Jews was provided by Cohen and Eisen (2000) in their volume *The Jew Within*. Their study, as its title suggests, pointed to the extent to which the meaning of Judaism increasingly transpires within the self rather than within the kinds of institutions that in previous generations marked out the contours of the organized Jewish community.

In a widely quoted paragraph, the authors write:

> More and more, the meaning of Judaism in America transpires
> within the self. American Jews have drawn the activity and sig-
> nificance of their group identity into the subjectivity of the
> individual, the activities of the family, and the few institutions
> (primarily the synagogue) which are seen as extensions of this
> intimate sphere. At the same time, relative to their parents'
> generation, today's American Jews in their thirties, forties, and
> early fifties are finding less meaning in mass organizations,
> political activity, philanthropic endeavor, and attachment to
> the state of Israel. In broad strokes, that which is personally
> meaningful has gained at the expense of that which is people-
> hood-oriented. (183–84)

Paradoxically, while others blamed the privatization of religious
life for the decline in church membership, Cohen and Eisen
argued that the inward turn they charted enhanced the synagogue's appeal, at least for those who didn't maintain membership
out of some recidivist corporate loyalty. This seems to explain
why subsequent evidence has indicated that congregations have
been more successful in recent years at attracting members who
participate with some frequency than they have been at ensuring
that families who rarely attend maintain their membership
(Wertheimer 2005). In the United States in the 1950s, an estimated
60 percent of American Jews belonged to a synagogue at some
point in time, while only 17–20 percent claimed to attend services
at least once a month. In contrast, the 2000–2001 National Jewish
Population Survey found that 46 percent of American Jews are
synagogue members, while 27 percent say they attend services at
least once a month (Wertheimer 2005). As Eisen and Cohen (2000)
suggest, the synagogue is not where people come to encounter
God, nor is it (if they are nonattending members) where they sig-
nal affiliation with some vague notion of Jewish community; it is
where they come "out of family interest . . . to be in palpable community . . . to soothe and nourish the harried self" (190). If they
don't find that the synagogue answers their needs in this way, then
they see little need to maintain membership.

What Cohen and Eisen (2000) say little about, either here or elsewhere in their study, is which institutions other than the synagogue might successfully connect with adults inclined to look for and find meaning close to the family as an "extension of this intimate sphere." Indeed, they lead one to wonder if communal institutions can be capable of nurturing shared commitments for adults whose search for meaning is so personalized, private, and even idiosyncratic. What possibilities exist, for example, for connecting with adult Jews who don't even maintain synagogue memberships? If the synagogue does not answer their most fundamental needs, can any other public Jewish institution?

The Prism of the Particular

These were the kinds of questions that came to mind after we completed the five-month pilot phase of research at DJDS. Having found parents spending so much time engaged directly and indirectly with what went on in the school, we wondered whether we weren't observing the kind of shared Jewish passion and communal solidarity that Cohen and Eisen despaired of finding outside the synagogue. If the moderately affiliated Jews they interviewed left them pessimistic about the possibilities for sustaining Jewish solidarity through American Jewish communal institutions, then the even more minimally affiliated Jews we encountered in our fieldwork at a children's Jewish day school encouraged us to see how parents might come to develop public Jewish commitments and a sense of Jewish community. To paraphrase Berger, we wondered if for the parents at DJDS, most of whom maintained no formal connection with other Jewish institutions, the sacred canopy of Jewish religious life hadn't come to settle on their children's school.

After spending three years collecting data in and around DJDS, in this book we make sense of the adult relationships and commitments we found. Employing a case study approach, the book sheds light on patterns of adult behavior and ideas that others have identified in a generalized and decontextualized fashion, by telling the story of one case, that of a small, religiously pluralistic, private elementary Jewish day school in downtown Toronto. Although, as will be made clear later, the study also draws on comparative empirical data collected at a number of schools in the United States and Canada, at this book's heart is the story of a particular school and of the adults and children whose lives intersect there.

In certain respects DJDS is neither representative of day schools elsewhere, which tend to be religiously Orthodox in orientation, nor typical of most urban public schools, which are culturally and socioeconomically more diverse, larger, and often more poorly resourced. For some, then, the setting will seem almost exotic. Compared to most other Jewish day schools, the diversity of religious commitments, family structures, and socioeconomic backgrounds of the children will seem unusual. For those familiar with public schools in North American cities, where class sizes rarely dip below twenty-five and sometimes reach forty students and where it is not unusual for children to speak at least a dozen first languages in the same classroom, the school's small size, cultural homogeneity, and comfortable material circumstances might seem to hail from another, less socially complex time and place.

Yet, in other respects, and particularly in terms of the sociology of North American Jewish life, DJDS provides a representative and richly suggestive case. It is at the cusp of what some have suggested is one of the most significant developments in organized Jewish life since the Second World War (Ackerman 1989; Wertheimer 1999). We have written elsewhere about what these developments might imply:

> For most of the last century, the great majority of liberal Jews in North America, if they chose to provide their children with a formal Jewish education, opted to send them to religious supplementary schools. As Sarna has argued, this educational model provided a satisfactory solution to "the most fundamental problem of Jewish life: how to live in two worlds at once, how to be both American and Jewish, part of the larger society and apart from it" (Sarna 1998, 9). During the day children attended public schools along with their fellow citizens, and during evenings and weekends they sat alongside co-religionists in synagogue classrooms so as to be exposed to Jewish culture and tradition.

> In recent years, increasing numbers of liberal Jews have abandoned the public school system and have signed up their children for a parochial model of education in which they study a dual curriculum of Jewish and general studies in an all-day setting separate from non-Jewish students. It seems as if there has been a changed assessment of what it means to be Jewish in America. (Pomson, in press)

In the 1960s approximately sixty thousand children attended Jewish day school in the United States, representing less than 10 percent of the Jewish school age population (Della Pergola and Schmelz 1989). Today more than two hundred thousand children attend day school, nearly one-fourth of Jewish school-age children (Schick 2005). While the great majority of day-school students in both Canada and the United States were and still are enrolled in Orthodox schools, a significant proportion of total day-school growth over the last fifteen years can be attributed to the registration of children in non-Orthodox schools. Today, between one-fifth and one-fourth of the total day-school population attends non-Orthodox schools (Schick 2005). The first non-Orthodox day school in North America opened in 1951, some fifty years after the first Orthodox day school was established. Today there are more than 150 day schools either affiliated with non-Orthodox denominations or organized as pluralistic or non-denominational institutions, with an estimated student population of approximately forty-five thousand.

DJDS (we argue at greater length in the next chapter) is typical of the non-Orthodox day schools created during the last fifteen years. Reflecting a new and growing trend, the school is religiously pluralistic. All of the students are being raised as Jews, but many have parents with minimal attachments to the organized Jewish community. The school is located in a neighborhood where today there are few other Jewish institutions, even though this area was once home to a major concentration of Jews. The school was established with matching funds provided by a private Jewish foundation that over the last decade has helped launch more than forty such schools with the explicit intent of attracting children who would not otherwise attend a Jewish day school.

In fact, there is much about the parents, students, and teachers at DJDS that make them comparable to adults and children in numerous other public and private schools in North America. The majority of the parents are public school graduates, and many (paradoxically perhaps) are outspoken advocates for public education. Although they have selected a "special" school for their children, this is not because of any sense of special entitlement. In terms of its admissions policy, the school is not selective beyond the requirement that all children be raised as Jews. In all of the classrooms at DJDS there are children with a wide range of academic needs, family arrangements, and socioeconomic circumstances. About one-third of families do not pay full fees but receive a financial subsidy, with some paying a token sum of less than five hundred dollars a year. Thus, although this is a self-selecting group—a "value community" in the limited sense that all have selected the same educational institution for their children and generally regard themselves in one sense or another as "downtown" types—these families came to the school with a wide variety of purposes and resources, means and ends. It is more appropriate to describe the parent body as a "functional community," that is, as exhibiting a degree of uniformity and cohesion within a mix of geographic, social, and economic boundaries. But even then, many if not most parents would not have known one another if their children had not been enrolled in the school (Coleman and Hoffer 1987).

As Alan Peshkin observed of a number of "exceptional" schools he chose to study, we believe that it is possible to learn something at DJDS that transcends its particular circumstances (2001, xi). But in order to confirm that the case of DJDS is neither peculiarly Canadian nor unusually dependent on the school's newness, we tell the story of the families at DJDS against the backdrop of data we collected from some two hundred further interviews with parents and teachers at six other Jewish day schools—two in Toronto and four in the pseudonymously named Centreville, a medium-sized city in the American Midwest. The Centreville data was collected by Pomson as part of a separately conceived study conducted during the same period of time as the Toronto research and provides a useful point of reference against which to compare the findings from DJDS (Pomson 2007). This data will be cited when relevant, but more typically it will provide a discrete frame for the ethnographic portrait painted of life at DJDS.

Methodologies Employed and Their Grounds

As indicated earlier, this inquiry proceeds from a view of identity and culture as constantly being made, unmade, and remade. In methodological terms it calls, therefore, not for a survey and summary of the modes of parental involvement but for the interpretation of parental interventions in terms of their significance for those who carry them out. We are interested in learning how agents offer an account of themselves and in figuring out what events mean for those who participate in them. We therefore use the ethnographic tools of interview and observation to help us determine what an event "says" and what people mean by what they say. In these terms interviews are performances to be observed and interpreted, and events are texts to be read and decoded (Tierney and Dilley 2002).

The range of meanings that an instance of parent involvement might possess is seen in the following example:

Parents often come in to school on a Friday afternoon to help organize the weekly "kabbalat Shabbat" (Sabbath preparation) program in the lower grades. This is an activity that re-creates in the classroom a ritual that for centuries Jews practiced in synagogues and homes. In contemporary Jewish schools it usually involves parent volunteers filling small plastic cups with grape juice (wine is out of the question on school premises, as is the use of valuable silverware), preparing ritual objects for use, helping children get settled in the classroom, and singing some songs along with the teacher. When parents offer to help conduct this weekly activity, they might intend to assist teachers in managing a labor-intensive activity, much as they would by volunteering to listen to individual children read or by chaperoning a school trip. Parents may also be interested in spending time with one of their own children with whom they otherwise have limited time together, at a time of the week when they have fewer work commitments. In short, they may be inspired by unexceptional if not predictable motivations for getting involved in their child's school and will be little affected by an event that happens week-in, week-out in the lower grades of most Jewish schools.

By involving themselves in this event, parents may, however, have different purposes: they may be seeking an opportunity to become more familiar with a ritual (reciting blessings over wine and bread, reciting prayers and songs) with which they have little familiarity. Indeed, it may be that it is only as a result of their participation in this classroom ritual that they learn enough about how to conduct this ceremony in their own homes or that they are inspired to do so, particularly when as adults they might be reluctant to attend a class in "basic Judaism" intended to teach "late starters" about such things.

The significance and value of an event such as this is not determined only by observation, no matter how acute. It calls for the careful questioning of participants—parents, teachers, and children—so as to learn about their purposes and experiences. In order to uncover these layers of meaning in the interactions between parents and the school, we conducted two semistructured interviews with all fourteen sets of DJDS parents who were new to the school in the academic year 2003–4. We first interviewed parents soon after their children joined the school and again eighteen months later. We also interviewed fourteen sets of "old-timer" parents, all of whose children were in one of the school's oldest grades in 2003 and who had been associated with the school for at least four years. So as to better understand the particularities of DJDS families, we interviewed a comparative sample of twenty further sets of parents whose children started school during the same period at two well-established Jewish day schools in the city: one, Ben Gurion, a secular Jewish school a couple of miles away in the city's midtown, and the other, Rav Kook, a coeducational Orthodox school in the city's suburbs. This comparison was intended to provide a better sense of who DJDS parents are and how they conceive of their relationships both with their children's school and with the Jewish community. In the pseudonymously named Centreville in the U.S. Midwest, further interviews were conducted with samples of more than eighty parents and teachers from all four Jewish elementary schools in the city, Leo Baeck Academy (a recently created Reform day school), the Frankel School (a Solomon Schechter–affiliated Conservative day school), the Hirsch Academy (a more than fifty-year-old modern-Orthodox day school), and the Hafetz Haim School (an ultra-Orthodox day school founded some fifteen years previously).

At DJDS we interviewed all teachers, administrators, and staff who work in the school at least half-time. We wanted to learn from them about their relationships with parents and also how they interpreted the interactions between parents and the school. Finally, we conducted interviews and focus groups with all of the children in one of the eldest elementary grades during the 2003–4 academic year and again the following year. We were interested in connecting what children said about school with the ways in which their parents talk. In a triangulating move, we were also interested in what they made of their parents' relationships with the school.

In all of these instances, interviews were given shape by observations in numerous school settings—in classrooms and during meetings, standing committees of the board, and special events where we observed parents, teachers, and children interacting with one another. We collected copies of all communications between the school and parents (weekly newsletters, special announcements, parent handbooks) as well as the minutes and written communications from a variety of school committees on which parents sit. We employed observations and document analysis in an attempt to trace the influence of parents on school events and school practices where they were not immediately present. During interviews with parents we looked for clues in their talk that pointed to the influence of the school on how they organize and express their ideas. In our account we have employed pseudonyms for all individuals and institutions other than DJDS.

Structure of the Book

In the following chapter we first provide a snapshot of the school and its ethnographic context, what it looks like as a pluralistic

Jewish day school, how the curriculum differs from a typical public school and from other Jewish day schools, the physical setting,
and the main characters present in the building. In chapter 2 we
try to make sense of what draws adults to the school when they
otherwise express a sharp and generalized ambivalence about
parochial schools. We find that a significant factor in their choice
is their search for an institution that can satisfy some of their
own personal and social needs as Jewish adults. In chapter 3 we
explore the ways in which parents are involved in the school and
exercise influence over its life once their children are registered.
Again, we discover that parental involvement—like their choice
of school in the first place—is often driven by deep personal concerns that go beyond their children's educational needs.

In the chapters that follow we explore the consequences and
implications of the relationships and impulses described in chapters 2 and 3. First, in chapter 4, we take up ethnographic tools to
explore the ways in which, for parents, the school takes on functions previously performed for adults by the synagogue as *bet
kenesset*, *bet midrash*, and *bet tephilah*. This is a phenomenon
we refer to as the "school as shul." Then, in chapter 5, we examine how parents also come into direct contact with school life—
at home, through the mediation of their own children—with no
less significant consequences for their own adult lives.

In the final chapters we investigate, first, whether the findings
collected at DJDS are replicated in other more conventional day-
school environments in both Canada and the United States.
Then, in the concluding chapter, this comparison allows us to
discuss how to imagine the cultivation of Jewish identity and
community in a postmodern context and how to conceive the
role of day schools in the lives of Jewish adults within a sociological context of changed patterns of Jewish identification.

A School Downtown

THE ETHNOGRAPHIC CONTEXT
FOR THE STUDY

A Jewish School Downtown

If you stand at the intersection of Toronto's Bloor and Spadina streets you can imagine yourself in any number of North American cities. A short distance away, glass-plated office towers, owned by banks and multinational companies, dominate the skyline. A few blocks down the street the familiar logos of major stores hang above the heads of pedestrians. Flagship outlets compete for the attention of tourists who will likely find the same stores in their hometowns, if on a smaller scale. At the Bloor-Spadina intersection itself, homeless people stand outside the 7–11 store trying to sell alternative newspapers to people who hurry past to the adjacent subway station. On most days, even in the heart of winter when the temperature doesn't rise above the freezing point for weeks, desperate individuals can be found making up beds in nearby doorways or on the heating grates above the subway.

On the southwest corner of the intersection, backing onto a field owned by Ontario's oldest university, is an institution that predates most of the neighboring stores and hotels. Known today as the Miles Nidal Jewish Community Centre, it was founded in 1919 as the Hebrew Literary and Athletic Club, a name that testifies to the mix of cultural and sporting functions that still provide its raison d'être. During the 1970s, 1980s, and 1990s, the Centre fell on hard times, the facility decaying, as membership dropped from a peak of 7,500 to less than 1,500. This decline was testament to a suburban drift not only among the Jewish community but also among other upwardly mobile ethnic groups, many of whose members were also registered at the club.

Today, when one walks through the doors of the Centre, there is little evidence of this recent troubled past. Instead, thanks to a Jewish community–funded renovation program completed in 2004, one encounters a modern, aesthetically appealing sports and cultural complex that serves a neighborhood that for the last couple of decades has been gradually gentrified and has seen for the first time in fifty years the Jewish population rebound to about twenty thousand. The building's lower floors are occupied by a number of lounges, a well-maintained swimming pool and gymnasium, and a good-sized auditorium in use most days of the week.

Upstairs on the second floor, beyond intruder-proof security doors and above the busy branch of the Second Cup café that does business across the corridor from the auditorium, one can find an institution that seems incongruous in this downtown sports and cultural center. Barely noticeable from the street, the second floor of the building is occupied by a K–6 elementary school whose classrooms run the length of the building's eastern facade. The "school yard" is three floors up, on the building's roof, protected by high fencing but blessed with stunning views of the city's skyline and the lake beyond. One suspects that many Centre members showering in the building's basement are not even aware of the educational activities that take place above their heads. After all, until the school opened in 1998, there hadn't been an all-day Jewish school in this part of the city for more than forty years.

The school—known as the Paul Penna Downtown Jewish Day School (DJDS)—was launched by a small group of pioneer parents who, in contrast to most of their own parents and siblings, had chosen to settle close to or within the city's downtown area. The school they launched in 1998 opened with a staff of three and just ten students. In 2002, when we started our research, there were seventy students in five grades, from senior kindergarten to grade 4, with class sizes ranging between twenty-three in the kindergarten to eight in grade 5. By 2006, when we completed our fieldwork, there were 101 students from senior kindergarten to grade 6, with a middle school projected to open the following year.

Between the Particular and the General

In order to best appreciate the nuances of life at DJDS, it is necessary to provide an account of the particular educational and communal context in which the school exists and of the extent to which it is similar to and different from the context surrounding other Jewish day schools in Toronto and North America. Disclosing the particular characteristics of the research setting in this way is not intended to emphasize the difference between DJDS and other schools; it is aimed instead at helping readers locate our findings in relation to other places and other times. To put it differently, the context we detail in this chapter is not intended to set up the study as a counterfactual case that indicates what could not happen elsewhere because it happens in the special circumstances at DJDS (Tetlock and Belkin 1996). As was previously suggested, the parents and families at DJDS have much in common with children and adults in other Jewish day-school settings, but because of special factors in the environment at DJDS, aspects and outcomes of their relationships are much more visible here. To that extent, the impulse behind this study is ethnographic. It makes it possible to describe features of day-school life that may be present in many school cultures but may not otherwise be easily visible.

One of the most significant statements that can be made about the communal and educational context in which DJDS is located is that at the time of its creation the school was one of more than twenty Jewish day schools at the elementary level in Toronto. In that city, with a population of more than three million and a Jewish community numbering about two hundred thousand, more than a third of Jewish school-age children attend all-day Jewish schools, a rate among the highest in any North American city and more than 50 percent higher than the norm across the United States. The student body at DJDS therefore constitutes a small part of the more than 11,500 students in Jewish day schools at the elementary and high school levels across the city.

The reasons for the high rates of day-school attendance in Toronto vary. In general terms, and as repeatedly confirmed by social-scientific research, Canadian Jews are more traditional in their Jewish behaviors than are American Jews (Brodbar-Nemzer et al. 1993). As Shaffir and Weinfeld put it, Canadian Jews "provide their children with more intensive Jewish education, make higher per-capita contributions and relatively more visits to Israel, are more likely to be Orthodox and less likely to be Reform, and have lower rates of intermarriage" (1981, 13). More specifically, in Toronto, the Jewish community came of age during the aftermath of the Second World War, under the leadership of a generation of Holocaust survivors who devoted, over many decades, a high level of funding to the development of an infrastructure for Jewish day schools. The city is also home to a sizable, provincially funded Catholic school system that has made it less controversial for Jewish parents to withdraw from public schools than was the case for many decades in the United States. Finally, since the 1980s there has been an influx into Toronto of young Anglophone Jewish families, many of them day-school graduates, who migrated from Montreal following the turbulence of the secession referenda in Quebec. These families have been strongly inclined to send their children to parochial Jewish schools.

DJDS shares these circumstances with other Toronto day schools but differs most sharply from them in that, while other Toronto day schools are typically suburban, located in sprawling middle-class neighborhoods with sizable Jewish populations served by extensive networks of Jewish institutions, DJDS is located in a downtown milieu where there are few visible Jewish institutions and where the population is more culturally diverse than in almost every other North American city. In these respects the school differs considerably from the two additional Toronto day schools we adopted as comparative field sites. One, the Rav Kook School, a modern-Orthodox day school created toward the end of the 1980s as a breakaway from a long-established day school, is located outside the city's municipal boundaries in one of the most densely populated Jewish neighborhoods in the province. The other, the Ben Gurion School, a secular Jewish day school founded at the start of the 1960s by Yiddishist Holocaust survivors, is situated beyond the downtown core in a comfortable neighborhood that was one of the city's first suburbs and where some of Canada's best-known synagogues can be found.

Unusual as the origins and orientation of DJDS may be within the Toronto context, the school is representative of an emerging trend in contemporary North American life. As indicated in the introduction, the school was established with matching funds provided by a private foundation with the explicit intent of attracting children from among the estimated five thousand Jewish children living downtown who would not otherwise attend a Jewish day school. Over the last decade, this same foundation has helped launch more than forty other such schools in a variety of geographic locations, most of which cater to a population of religiously non-Orthodox Jewish students who, twenty years previously, were found in only very small numbers in parochial Jewish schools. Thanks to the involvement of this foundation, there are today "downtown" day schools like DJDS in Brooklyn, Chicago, and Washington, D.C., in urban settings once heavily populated by Jews but only recently repopulated by Jewish families disaffected with denominational Jewish life in the suburbs.

Day Schools in American Suburbia

The suburban denominational day school constitutes the paradigm case against which to appreciate the significance of what schools like DJDS imply for the future of Jewish life in North America. In the pages that follow we compare the families at DJDS not only to those at the Rav Kook and Ben Gurion schools in Toronto but also to those from four Jewish day schools in the pseudonymously named city of Centreville in the U.S. Midwest. What makes the day schools of Centreville so useful as points of comparison to DJDS is how different they are from it in their location, genesis, and affiliation, and yet how similar they are to it in the ways many parents talk about their relationship to these schools and in how the schools serve as the locus for parents' Jewish lives, particularly for the religiously non-Orthodox among them.

To introduce Centreville briefly: the city has a population of slightly more than 2.5 million and is home to some sixty thousand Jews, almost all of whom have moved out of the inner city into the suburbs of Centreville County where their numbers have been stable for the last thirty years. The Jewish community supports four different elementary day schools spanning the denominational spectrum, with a combined population of almost 650 students.

Centreville's four day schools, and the timing of their creation, correspond well with trends that have played out across the United States over the last fifty years. The Hirsch Academy (a pseudonym as are the names of the other Centreville schools we studied) was founded in the 1940s under Orthodox auspices with a goal of serving students from across the community. It is one of the oldest American day schools outside the eastern seaboard. In the early 1980s a second day school, the Frankel School, was launched under the aegis of the Conservative Solomon Schechter day school network during a period that coincided with a bitter desegregation battle in Centreville-area public schools. In the late 1980s a third school, Hafetz Haim Prep, was launched by a group of parents who split from the Hirsch Academy in order to create an ultra-Orthodox non-coeducational school for boys and girls. Most recently, in the late 1990s, a Reform school, the Leo Baeck Academy, was founded with the help of matching funds from the same foundation that made possible the launch of DJDS.

The proportion of Jewish children enrolled in Centreville day schools is below the U.S. average of 20 percent, reflecting the higher level of affiliation with Reform congregations in the city than in other parts of the country. At the same time, there is a long history among Centreville's general population of above-average enrollment in private schools because of the prominence of European immigrants with a preference for Catholic education. A protracted legal battle over school desegregation climaxing in the 1980s has also contributed to a general erosion of confidence in public education in the suburban neighborhoods of Centreville where most Jews live. These factors all contribute to the general stability of the city's four suburban Jewish day schools.

A Downtown State of Mind

If we have belabored the contrast between the suburban milieu of the other six schools where we collected data and the downtown location of DJDS, it is because, for many at DJDS and in the wider community as well, the school's downtown setting is not merely a geographic fact. Being downtown means that the school serves a community without recent close access to day-school education; more profoundly, it is indicative also of where the school is located in the city's social and cultural landscape. As one of the school's early promotional brochures puts it, "Living and learning downtown implies a commitment to diversity, an openness to what the city has to offer, and pluralism in action."

Although this characterization is highly idealized, it is by no means inaccurate. This construction of "downtownness" shapes how many in the school talk about themselves and the institution. As Jewish day schools go, DJDS exhibits unusual openness to nontraditional family structures: more than a quarter of the children in the school have parents who are intermarried, the same sex, or single. This is in contrast to the majority of Jewish day schools in North America, where parents must demonstrate that they conform to certain normative Jewish family structures. There is also no doubting the school's commitment to religious and ideological pluralism. This is evidenced, for example, in its progressive curriculum that places a strong emphasis on the integration of Jewish and general studies, its inclusive classroom practice that seeks to cater to children with diverse learning needs and interests, and its liberal staffing policy: teachers are not required to affiliate with any particular Jewish denomination or to teach according to any particular set of Jewish tenets. According to its mission statement the school seeks to build a pluralistic and tolerant community through integrating "Jewish and secular studies while encouraging artistic expression as a tool of learning" (DJDS mission statement 2000). These goals communicate a vision for Jewish education that is distinct from that of most other day schools, which are usually tied to the beliefs and practices of particular denominational groups. In Centreville, for example, all four day schools are affiliated with particular Jewish denominations, even if—with the exception of Hafetz Haim Prep, the ultra-Orthodox school—these schools are ready to admit children from relatively diverse Jewish backgrounds.

Families

With few exceptions, DJDS families live in and around the city's downtown core, an area that is home to extremes of wealth and poverty. In socioeconomic terms, the school's diversity is seen not so much in wealth (about 20 percent of students in fact receive subsidies toward the annual fee of more than $12,000) as it is in the different ways parents are employed. While the parent body contains no small number of lawyers and accountants, there are many more parents who work in the creative arts (dance, film, design, music), intellectual professions (journalism, psychiatry, higher education), and welfare services (nursing, education, social work). The school's board is unusual in including, at one time, a pastry chef, a costume designer, and a national newspaper editor—all of whom have children in the school.

This is a highly educated—one might say, intellectual—group, many of whom have been attracted to the downtown area because of its proximity to cultural institutions and to a major North American university. For a group of private school parents, they seem relatively lacking in materialism. As one teacher put it: "For these parents what is important is more the kinds of kids they have than the things their kids have."

In some respects, DJDS parents differ markedly from typical Jewish day-school parents. They are less interested in buying houses with large backyards than in access to public transit and a sense of neighborhood. A surprising number neither own cars nor know how to drive. They tend to be older too. They started their families late, often in their late thirties and into their forties, and have few children—most have only one or two. A small number have adopted children, which explains the presence of children of color in the school.

For most parents, living downtown expresses an intent to disengage from organized and denominational Jewish life. This is a part of town where few Jewish organizations have a presence. Only about half of the parents hold memberships at Jewish institutions other than at the "downtown JCC" where the school itself is located. Conventionally, social scientists view synagogue membership as a primary indicator of Jewish communal connection. Yet, while some 85 percent of day-school parents in Toronto (and 95 percent in the United States) currently maintain synagogue membership, only 50 percent do so at DJDS, and a quarter of these are members of what Wertheimer (2005) would call a "progressive niche synagogue," a local fellowship where Jews band together periodically for prayer and other activities. Those parents who attend services at synagogues tend to prefer the style at a local "traditional egalitarian" service rather than in one of the denominational congregations in the city's midtown neighborhoods. Others prefer to develop their own rituals either within their own immediate families or with close friends. In this respect, these families vividly exemplify the phenomenon of "believing without belonging" to which we referred in the previous chapter and which we found to be common among non-Orthodox day-school families both in Toronto and in Centreville. What this means in practice is explained by one DJDS mother:

> We still feel connected to our Judaism but not necessarily in the traditional way, a little more secular. Neither of us like synagogue, we haven't really found a place that we like to go as a family, and our kids completely hate it and we don't want to make them go. . . . So we sometimes do go to Shaarei Chesed [a Conservative synagogue] sometimes to be with John's father in respect to him. . . . Otherwise on Rosh Hashanah we like to apple orchard, and to have our own family ceremonies as well. We sit in the orchard and talk about what our new year's resolutions are and we will go around and say what we want to do. . . . Or on Yom Kippur we go to a ravine and we ask for forgiveness from one another. We do things that are personally meaningful. . . . Generally, it is the six of us doing it together. . . . Our neighbor wanted to come with us this year, she is like a surrogate aunt. She is not Jewish but she is a surrogate aunt; so she came with us. (Jean Richards)

Strikingly, given that parents have selected a parochial Jewish school for their children, none seem interested in living in neighborhoods where there are many other Jewish families. Whereas the parents we interviewed at the Ben Gurion School typically chose to live in neighborhoods where they "wouldn't be the only Jews" or that "were a good mix, not totally Jewish," and whereas

Rav Kook School families lived only in predominantly Jewish neighborhoods, DJDS parents sought out areas of town that were socioeconomically and culturally diverse and where, in many cases, they were the only Jewish family on the street.

Faculty

As is often the case in new schools, there has been considerable turnover of faculty during the school's first seven years, even as a small number of teachers have remained with the school since its beginning. The founding principal, Jessica Steinberg, an experienced educator, served in a part-time role during the school's first three years while continuing to act as the principal of a local part-time Hebrew school she founded more than twenty years previously. Deeply committed to the success of DJDS and to the development of the downtown Jewish community, her involvement was something of an emergency measure to help get the school started.

In the school's second year, Jessica was joined by Cheryl Levin, another experienced educator, who served as part-time vice principal and curriculum coordinator for three years. Cheryl left the school a year before the start of our research and one year after the appointment of Jessica's successor, but her influence is still evident as the architect of the school's distinctive approach to the integration of Jewish and general studies. Cheryl was succeeded by two further vice principals, one who stayed with the school for just a year and another who stayed for two years.

Erica Caplin, Jessica's successor as principal, was starting her second year in the position when we began our research. A native Torontonian, a graduate of local Jewish day schools, and a single mother, Erica commuted to the school every day from the suburbs. This was her first position as a school principal following a number of years in the classroom in Israel and in Canada.

By the time we finished our three years of research at the school, and following a period of some turbulence, Erica had also left the school to be replaced by Sandra Meyers, an experienced teacher who was closer in age and religious orientation to most of the parents than was her predecessor. Sandra was promoted to the position of principal after having been appointed as a classroom teacher during the previous year to take up an unexpectedly vacant position.

In 2002, when we started our research, there were at the school six full-time faculty members apart from Erica Caplin; a vice principal and a business manager, both of whom worked four days a week; three half-time Hebrew language specialists; and additional part-time specialists in art, music, French, and physical education. The full-time faculty served as homeroom teachers in each grade and were responsible for teaching the core general studies curriculum as well as those parts of the Judaic studies program not taught in Hebrew. Two of the six full-time teachers had been with the school since it opened, although one had taken a year off to complete a full-time masters degree.

Students

The students at DJDS may lack the linguistic and cultural diversity of the student population in other downtown schools, but in comparison to other Toronto Jewish day schools, and even to most other private schools, this group can comfortably be labeled as diverse. In fact, celebrating (and not merely coping with) diversity is at the heart of life and learning in the school. This means that more or less every student is able to articulate in which way he or she is unique. Similarly, these students can articulate the common grounds on which they have been educated to be respectful, caring Jewish members of their downtown neighborhood.

The expression and celebration of each student's uniqueness is one of the features of the school that newcomers first observe. This is well demonstrated by a piece Sandra Meyers wrote in the school's weekly newsletter in which she connected this feature to what she learned from one of her early experiences at DJDS.

> This week, I greeted parents who are considering our school for their child. During these meetings I always come around to asking why they are considering our school, for I always find it interesting to hear how others understand us. The answers vary, but often there is a reference to the appeal of a school

where each child's uniqueness is valued. This comment fills me
with great pride, but also with trepidation. What an enormous
task and responsibility—to value each child's uniqueness!

I remember my first week as a teacher at DJDS. One of my
grade 5 students arrived in a pink tutu, fairy wings, and a fluffy
wand. Had I not been told about a special theme day? No one
else seemed to be dressed up. No one else even seemed to
notice that this student was dressed up. When I asked her about
her get-up she simply stated that it represented her mood that
day, and the school day began. At that moment I knew I had
found a wonderful place.

Another striking feature of the students is that they demonstrate
highly developed expressive skills. Their teachers suggest that
this is a result of the school's emphasis on creating concrete connections between learned topics, student life past and present,
and multiple modes of expression such as art, music, and creative
writing. It is likely also that the advanced levels of student
expression reflect the often intense intellectual environment in
the students' homes, a quality associated, one suspects, with the
school's downtown location.

More typical of students in other schools, DJDS students favor
recess over learning classroom "subjects." Unlike in other schools,
however, they are encouraged to bring back from recess into
the classroom issues of friendship, justice, and honesty. These
issues are not only discussed but integrated into topics of study,
often making these topics more relevant and the conflicts more
amenable to resolution.

Governance

Like almost all Jewish day schools in North America, DJDS is privately incorporated and is operated as a not-for-profit organization. It is governed by an eighteen-member board of directors. A
minimum of 30 percent of the directors must be parents. The balance of the board is made up of parents and community members,
some of whom (including some of the parent members) are not

Jewish. In contrast to many other Jewish day schools, the DJDS board does not include representation from local synagogues or from the federated Jewish community and its board of education. Although in the most general terms this is a parochial school, the school is not actually affiliated with any "parish" or synagogue.

According to the school's parent handbook, the board of directors is the legal entity that is ultimately responsible for the school. It is the board's responsibility to hire the principal, who in turn is responsible for the day-to-day activities of the school. The handbook further emphasizes that because of the school's newness, and the consequent challenge of meeting many costs not covered by tuition fees, fund-raising is one of the board's primary responsibilities.

A parents' association also operates at the school. As explained by the parent handbook, it was created "to serve the needs of the entire school community." Although the parents' association president sits on the school board, the association is not a body that sets policy. Again, as emphasized by the handbook, its primary function, as exercised through numerous subcommittees, is to "give support and feedback . . . to the teachers and administration."

Policies and Procedures

Admissions. Any child being raised at home as a Jew is eligible for admission to the school, regardless of the affiliation, observance, and faith of parents. This policy accords with the school's stated commitment to religious pluralism, characterized in the parent handbook as a commitment to "respect the divergent modes of Jewish belief and practice, and [to] welcome children from a broad spectrum of Jewish backgrounds, from secular to traditional." Admission is organized on a first-come, first-served basis, although all applicants are required to participate in an entrance interview that helps determine whether the school can cater to a child's academic, social, and personal needs.

Tuition and subsidies. First-time applicants to the school must make out a $500 nonrefundable deposit to the school. For the 2005–6 academic year, the full fee for a first child was a further $11,350. Each additional child was eligible for a $250 reduction. The payment could be made over an eight-month period, and a tax receipt (for 63 percent of paid tuition) was available to parents.

All students are eligible to receive a subsidy toward the cost of tuition following an internally administered needs assessment. During the 2003–4 academic year, subsidies were awarded to 20 percent of students on a range from $3,800 to $10,487.

Behavior, dress, and dietary codes. The parent handbook includes a code of behavior that specifies the entitlements and expectations for children, staff, and parents. Parents are not required to sign the code, but the handbook explains that the code's purpose is "to clearly outline for all partners at DJDS the expectations we have of each of other" and to "ensure that the parents/staff/children view the Jewish school as a center of learning which has as part of its core philosophy a spirit of mutual respect (*derech eretz*) regardless of race, ancestry, place of origin, color, ethnic origin, citizenship, religion, religious practice, gender, sexual orientation, age or disability."

In contrast to many other Jewish day schools, the dress code does not require that students wear school uniforms. The only limitation is that girls can and boys must cover their heads at all times in line with traditional Jewish custom. Like most other Jewish schools, there is also a dietary policy, which in this case, "in order to accommodate the many levels of *kashrut* observed by members of the DJDS community," requires that children only bring into school food that is either dairy or parve (neither meat nor dairy) so as to prevent the mixing of meat and milk food products as forbidden by traditional Jewish dietary law. Food from home cannot be shared either. These policies nicely codify the mix of pressures and concerns that emerge from the school's commitment to religious pluralism. Families are not required to keep kosher (and in fact hardly any do), nor are they required to bring specifically kosher products into the school. The policy as formulated, while frustrating to some by limiting what they can give their children for lunch, does specifically avoid religious coercion and establishes a threshold that allows the minority of families who do keep kosher to feel comfortable in the school.

Statements of the School's Philosophy

Like many other alternative schools, an elaborate educational philosophy has been developed at DJDS to give direction to what is essentially a countercultural project. The ideas that animate the school's existence and activity have been stated in a variety of forms. In most concentrated fashion, they have been expressed as a series of commitments that appear in a variety of school publicity materials. These are stated as commitments to "academic excellence with a love of learning; creativity and artistic expression; a meaningful Jewish identity; caring and a sense of responsibility for the world and its people; and respect for diversity within the Jewish and Canadian communities."

Stated so succinctly, these commitments are not especially distinctive. A commitment to "academic excellence" or to developing "a meaningful Jewish identity" would be promised at pretty much any Jewish day school, and "respect for diversity within the Jewish and Canadian communities" might only be contentious in an ultra-Orthodox day school. The particular educational orientation at DJDS is therefore seen more clearly in a carefully articulated statement of mission and vision that describes these commitments more thoroughly:

> The DJDS is the Jewish day school that serves the core of the City of Toronto. It is committed to academic excellence in a warm, supportive environment. Classes are small, ensuring personal attention for each child. The DJDS's distinctive program integrates Jewish and secular studies while encouraging artistic expression as a tool for learning.
>
> A central theme of studies at the DJDS is the moral and spiritual development of its students. Its curriculum encourages the importance of Jewish unity and continuity. The school embraces the values of equality and diversity, where boys and girls equally participate in all aspects of the DJDS curriculum.

Students of all Jewish family and spiritual backgrounds are fully accepted members of our community.

By dedicating itself to each child's intellectual, moral and emotional growth, the DJDS offers its students the opportunity to meet their full potential as individuals, Jews and valued members of the larger community.

A few elements in this statement are worth noting, particularly where they depart from usual practice in Jewish day schools: All Jewish day schools in North American deliver a dual curriculum of Jewish (or Hebrew) studies and general studies. Most schools make a clear separation between the two parts of the curriculum but allocate different proportions of time to their delivery. Some divide the day equally: non-Orthodox schools tend to devote more time to general studies, and more strictly Orthodox schools devote more time to Jewish studies. (In fact, five out of the six other schools we studied organize their curriculum around this fundamental division.) But DJDS, like a small number of other progressive schools such as the Leo Baeck Academy in Centreville, integrates the Jewish and general curriculum. In other words, elements from the Judaic and general studies curriculum are taught in an interrelated fashion in the same classroom by the same teacher. In staffing terms, this orientation places particular pressure on the school, as multiqualified teachers must be found who are capable and comfortable with teaching "across the curriculum." In philosophical terms, however, this arrangement gives expression to an educational goal of nurturing within students the capacity to think holistically and associatively by connecting Jewish ideas and values to the wider world.

Integration of Jewish values and ideas within the larger world is seen also in the school's commitment to the "core of the City of Toronto." If such concerns hardly seem noteworthy, they are worth contrasting with the intent of the pioneers of Jewish day-school education in North America who saw the all-day Jewish school as a fortress that would help children avoid being overwhelmed by the world outside. From the perspective of critics, this was why Jewish day schools were "undemocratic and unsocial" and represented a "withdrawal into a shell of separatism" (Dinin 1933; Reichert 1951; both cited in Drachler 1996). At

DJDS, as at a growing number of Jewish day schools, parochial education does not imply parochialism or cultural separatism but rather engagement with the world through the agency of a distinct minority culture.

Last, the stated commitment to equity and diversity, in terms of gender, academic ability, and religious belief, should not be taken lightly. In the vast majority of Jewish day schools, most of which are religiously Orthodox, boys and girls study separately, and in the higher grades their programs of study are organized around different content. While day schools do not tend to be academically selective, the demands of the dual curriculum of Jewish and general studies have meant that a certain self-selection occurs. Until the last decade when day schools started to invest in special education programs and resources, only students without learning difficulties were able to achieve success in the system. Finally, denominational schools, often affiliated with religious organizations, limit the diversity of students they admit. Many only accept students defined as halachically Jewish, that is, students whose mothers are Jewish. Some require students' families to be members of certain congregations. Few schools accept students whose parents are intermarried or openly gay, let alone encourage such families to be active in the school's governance. The commitment to equity and diversity as spelled out in the mission statement at DJDS is therefore of profound importance in shaping the culture at the school, particularly because these commitments establish the school's difference from typical Jewish day schools.

An Enactment of the School's Philosophy

The full significance of the ideas expressed in these statements is hard to appreciate in the abstract. A thicker sense of their consequence can be gained by reading a vignette composed by a member of the research team, Dafna Ross, during one of her visits to the school at the start of a typical winter's morning. In this account of morning prayers and a weekly spelling test, two activities that are part of the warp and woof of regular life in Jewish schools, one quickly sees the ways in which the curriculum and culture at DJDS differ from that usually seen in other schools, whether Jewish or not.

Field Notes, Grade 4, February 3, 2004

It's a winter Friday morning. The rush hour traffic and difficult weather don't help me get to school early enough. I enter the grade 4 class and apologize for being late. I confront a complete antithesis to my own rush. The children and the teacher are seated on the carpet in a circle, holding hands in a very serene way. The teacher welcomes the children to a new day in class. Apparently, this is their second activity of the day for upon entering the class they'd had "quiet work" time, in which they needed to choose either an independent activity in reading or math. I had seen this activity before and found it an effective transitional activity that enabled the kids to begin the day gradually and very leisurely.

Following the "welcome song" and still on the carpet, the students begin their daily morning prayer—done in every Jewish school, but here for each word said there is a hand movement created by the teacher so as to make the prayer a meaningful rather than mechanical ritual. I'm surprised that there is 100 percent participation. My previous day school experience prepared me for much less and, at best mechanical participation. Even Dan, who is usually busy playing with pencils, is now busily praying. Between each prayer there is a break, and a short discussion occurs whereby the teacher puts the prayer into context, states the main ideas and connects them to the children's own lives. For example, in praying for health, they mention the names of family members that are sick. . . . Similarly, the blessing for peace is followed by mention of conflicts in Israel and an incident of a conflict between two children. . . . The whole prayer session takes twenty minutes and seems to cover many areas. Beyond the words, movement, and discussion, I find the atmosphere of tranquility, respect, and interest inspiring.

From there the teacher draws the students to their weekly spelling test. While I am wondering how this routine activity will play within the context of the school, I am struck by the smooth transition between the two activities. I was ready for some release of energy that would perhaps be evident in a typical classroom, with a couple of children going to the washroom, the level of noise in the room rising, and refocusing by the teacher accordingly. It didn't happen. There wasn't total silence, but there was a very low and relaxed chatter as the kids rose and moved from the carpet to their desks. Again, the tranquility continues to amaze me. I ask the teacher, half-jokingly, whether many children are missing and she asks me why I'm asking such a question.

Soon enough the spelling test begins but the teacher conducts two different tests at the same time, one for the whole class and, while they are writing their words, she gives Dan, an ESL student, a different list of words. Again, I am surprised to see Dan's evident comfort. Even further, I watch the children's responses to the "easy" words he's given and anticipate some reaction. I don't see any, in fact the opposite. Dan seems to feel so secure that he is able to stop the teacher and ask for clarification. Two children from a different table jump up to help.

The spelling test continues and the children are focused. I am checking to see if they are looking at each others' notebooks or hiding them, but I don't see anything. As the test finishes the children are asked to follow the routine for checking and marking their test. They all seem to know what to do. They take out their books and give themselves two marks: one for correct answers and the second for the effort they put into achieving their score. I walk around and see each child work on his/her work without comparing or contrasting with classmates. When Dan asks for help, another child jumps to help. The teacher reminds them that this activity is personal.

As they finish, they come to put their notebook on the teacher's desk. They don't simply leave it there, but exchange and share their achievements with the teacher and she gives each one of them a handshake followed by a personal and specific reinforcement.

Beyond Context to the Content and Consequences of School Life for Parents

When we have read this extract at conferences and workshops, teachers gasp; they wonder aloud why their schools can't be like this, why they can't be as tranquil and suffused with meaning. Some tell us that situations like this are not so surprising when there are only fifteen children in the class, but that in their classes they have to cope with twenty-five or thirty-five students. In other words, they make a distinction between what takes place at DJDS and what takes place in their own schools, suggesting that few conclusions of relevance can be drawn from such an outlier case.

In this chapter we have tried to preempt such a conclusion. It is true that DJDS is a small school. It is home to a group of exceptional teachers. The school is also animated by a powerful and distinctive educational vision. But as we have tried to emphasize in a number of ways, the families who are attracted to the school are remarkably diverse, especially given the parochial setting; many are uncomfortable inside visibly Jewish institutions and are unfamiliar with much of Jewish culture. In these respects they more resemble those Jewish families who generally do not send their children to day school than those who do. As we see in this vignette, their children also possess diverse academic abilities, and they engage in activities that in a mundane sense are part of what Tyack and Tobin (1993) call the grammar of all schools. A first-time visitor to the school who had never before stepped inside a Jewish day school would find it an essentially familiar educational setting.

DJDS may be a special school, but it is not an exceptional school. And that is why it is so fertile a site for examining a set of relationships and associations that likely occur elsewhere but less visibly. It is to these relations that we now turn as we try to understand what at first brings families to the school, why they become involved in its life, and what the consequences are of their involvement.

The Winding Road to School

WHY AND HOW PARENTS CHOOSE DJDS

Conceptualizing (Day) School Choice

Scholars and commentators have interpreted the emerging popularity of schools like DJDS that serve a religiously liberal Jewish population as evidence of a sharp deterioration in the quality of public education, or at least as reflecting a perception of deterioration (Beinart 1999; Kelman 1984; Zeldin 1988). That liberal Jews, a minority group historically prominent as advocates for public education, have abandoned public schools for alternatives they regard as safer and academically more rigorous, provides evidence, it is said, of deepening disenchantment with public education if not public services more generally among the middle classes (Shapiro 1996).

In addition, the steady drift of liberal Jews toward parochial schools has been viewed as indicating a reassessment among Jews of their rights and obligations as a minority community in liberal democracies (Diamond 2000; Shrager 2002; Wertheimer 1999). As Sarna (1998) puts it, the turn to day schools suggests a different understanding of what it means to be Jewish in the United States (or anywhere else for that matter).

In this chapter we examine whether such grand claims can be made from the way parents at DJDS reflect on their choice of school. Drawing on interviews with all fourteen sets of parents whose children joined the school in September 2003, we see how and why they chose the school and how they conceive of their choice. When appropriate, we compare these responses with those of twenty further sets of parents whose children started school during the same period at the Ben Gurion School and at the Rav Kook School. This comparison provides a better sense of who DJDS parents are and how they conceive of their relationships both with their children's school and with the Jewish community. The comparison also builds a context for our inquiry into the relationships between DJDS parents and the school once children are enrolled.

Our approach to presenting data can be characterized as a kind of pointillist ethnography: we seek to compose a portrait of school choice from an aggregate of qualitative minutiae. We therefore quote directly and sometimes at length from interview transcripts in which parents talk about themselves and their choices. We also provide details of the educational backgrounds, socioeconomic circumstances, and religious and cultural practices of parents because these often play an important role in parents' decisions. By themselves, these quotations and vignettes are too particular and quirky to shed light on a larger set of phenomena. Close up they look like a series of unconnected points. Viewed together, however, they compose a vivid portrait of a cohort of families who for all their differences share a number of common concerns and experiences. It is our claim that a coherent picture of the journey to Jewish day school emerges from these many particulars.

A central challenge in studying school choice (as in much social scientific research) is to avoid reductionism, that is, the distillation of complex sets of considerations and constraints into a series of analytical categories that rarely correspond with the choices made by particular individuals at particular moments in time. In the case of day schools, reductionism often takes the form of depicting day-school choice as a matter of "push" and "pull," of parents either being in flight from unsatisfactory public school options or being drawn by deep(ening) Jewish commitments to a parochial Jewish school option. In the first instance, it is assumed that public school constitutes a default that parents (sensibly) abandon only when this option fails to meet their needs or expectations, or as one DJDS family put it, when "public schools scare the heck out of us." In the second instance, it is assumed that some families live within particular value communities where school choice is more or less determined by a larger set of social and personal commitments and associations. In these circumstances, such parents will say that they "don't have a choice" when it comes to their children's schooling even if they have access to an array of school options (Pomson 2007).

In order to steer between these two interpretative extremes— one overly rationalistic, the other overly deterministic—we take as the theoretical starting point for our investigation the work of those who have approached the study of school choice through the application of rational choice theory to an appreciation of the social context for decision making. Rational choice theory conceives of individuals as rational decision makers who act out of self-interest and who choose alternatives that provide the highest benefits based on individual preferences (Ostrom and Ostrom 1971). As Goldring and Shapira (1993) have explained, this theory implies that in the case of school choice, parents weigh various educational alternatives and make choices that maximize their own goals. Parents "reflect on their own values and on the needs of their own children and [then] articulate perceived preferences regarding education," having weighed their costs and benefits (397–98).

As Coleman (1990) made explicit nearly two decades ago, the problem with a rational choice perspective is that, although it corresponds to the native language individuals (parents) employ, people frequently do not weigh (schooling) alternatives in the context of accurate and adequate information. They rely on hearsay even when making decisions of great significance. They may simply not know all of their options. Moreover, no matter how independent minded individuals may claim to be, they do not make decisions in isolation from social contexts and social networks. These networks not only influence the quantity and quality of information on which individuals draw in order to make choices but also shape the values and commitments that determine how individuals act on this information, that is, how they prioritize considerations and concerns (Coleman and Hoffer

1987). These limitations do not therefore mean that people's decisions are narrowly determined, but they do imply that their decisions are made in negotiation with a complex web of given or inherited circumstances and constraints.

An Example of Complexity

The complexity of the school-choice process (and the inappropriateness of employing reductionist sociological models to account for it) is usefully demonstrated by the example of the Lowes, a DJDS family who talk frankly about the calculations and circumstances that brought them circuitously to the school.

As they see it, Adam and Karen Lowe are probably more affluent and more religiously observant than most other families at DJDS. Adam is a surgeon; Karen is a senior executive in a small commercial business. Married for ten years, they have always lived in neighborhoods close enough to the city center where they can manage without a car. This is true of where they live today; they are one of only a small number of Jewish families on a street leading to the edge of the city's midtown that they describe as especially neighborly. Although Adam is rarely home on Friday night (his operating night at the hospital), Karen makes a point of marking the Sabbath with the children: "We do the challah. We do the blessing over the grape juice and we do the candles. And we sing at least one song that Thomas every time he sees candles starts singing."

Both Adam and Karen attended Jewish day schools until grade 8; Adam in Montreal, Karen in Toronto. Although their siblings' children go to day school, neither of them were "of the mind" to send their own children. Karen, who deprecatingly characterizes herself as "a self-hating Jew," explains: "I didn't want [our children's] world to be too narrow. I didn't want them only to be friends with Jewish kids. . . . I don't like that kind of ghetto mentality I saw growing up. . . . I wanted them to have a much broader world. And I wanted to make sure also from an educational perspective that they weren't becoming fluent in Hebrew or Tanakh (Bible) or Talmud at the expense of something that might be a little bit more useful."

For these reasons they sent their oldest child, Carla, first to their local public school junior kindergarten, a multicultural setting with a reputation for warmth and affection, and then to a private Montessori senior kindergarten with excellent academics. At the same time, because "it was always important for our children to know that they were Jewish and to know what that meant to us and also to pass on what we hoped it would be to them," the family started to attend synagogue more frequently. Carla also began a Sunday Hebrew school program, first at the Downtown Community Centre and then at a synagogue. As Karen comments, although she and Adam are essentially loners who like to be with their children by themselves, "we thought, well maybe, that the synagogue is where the center of our Jewish life will be."

And yet, as Karen continues, "we found that once a week for two hours wasn't really sufficient" in terms of their goal of helping their children learn who they were Jewishly.

> Adam: Carla didn't like it. It was a hassle every Sunday to get her to school.
>
> Karen: She didn't really make any friends. . . . She is not a morning person so at the best of times to get her up and out of the house on a Sunday from nine to noon was hard. We both work during the week. We sort of felt like we weren't seeing her a lot. We let her skip whenever she had a birthday party or when we would go back to Montreal or Ottawa. I mean it got to the point where she was probably going once a month, maybe twice a month on good months. And then she began to resent it, I mean she began to say she didn't want to go to school on Sundays. You know, she was really enjoying having a baby brother and we thought we didn't want her to resent it. So that's when we started looking into day schools and we looked at a bunch of them.

In fact, Adam and Karen investigated two other day schools before they found DJDS almost by a process of elimination. Ben Gurion, their first choice on academic grounds, proved unfriendly and exclusive. Schechter, their second choice (Karen's alma mater), was friendly but seemed unprepared to deal with large class sizes of twenty-eight to thirty children. It was at the recommendation of an old friend of Adam's from Montreal that they came to the open house at DJDS.

Karen summarizes what appealed to them about the school:

> It was somewhat made for us in the sense that it was very
> urban. It was downtown-focused. It wasn't so homogenous
> with regard to the socioeconomic makeup. It was inclusive in
> that there were mixed marriages there. There were same-sex
> marriages there. You just got a real cross-section of what
> Judaism could be, and it seemed like it was Judaism without all
> the sort of the dogma about it. It wasn't political. It wasn't
> overly Zionistic or overly Israeli influenced, and the parents
> really had a say in how the school was developing. And I liked
> the class size. I thought the examples of the work that I saw
> were on a par with anything else that I had seen in other
> schools.

This combination of academic, ideological, and social factors persuaded them that DJDS was the right school for them, but as
Karen continues, other considerations were at work:

> Karen: I couldn't presume what other people's reasons are for
> sending their children there, but you know I suspect that like
> anybody else, you are all looking for somewhere to belong to
> some degree or another. And I think for a lot of the parent pop-
> ulation, they just, for whatever reason, either felt out of place at
> the other day schools or are just really committed to a down-
> town life. . . . It's funny, because I sometimes think that we
> stand out at DJDS because we are probably a little bit, I don't
> want to say, like more affluent, but a little bit more typical of
> what you might expect from day-school families.
>   Adam: But we wanted to be the minority.
>   Karen: Exactly. I didn't want to be surrounded by doctors,
> lawyers, and accountants, the financial guys. I wanted to have
> artists that sort of thing.

The specifics of the Lowes' journey to DJDS should not be taken
as typical of other new families in the school. Their account is
singled out here because of the articulate way both partners talk
about the mix of calculations (class size, social mix), contingen-
cies (their difficulties keeping a Sunday-school commitment), and
constraints (their determination to enable their children to pass
on Judaism) that brought them to the school. The consequences

of this mix are no more predictable in their case than they are for many other families in our sample. But their story is useful because it makes explicit issues that are common to other families, even if those issues are filled with different meaning for others. These issues, which we found surfacing across many if not most of our interviews with new parents, include (a) ambivalence about parochial Jewish schools, (b) the search for a quality education, (c) concern about children's Jewishness, and (d) anxiety about adult belonging and difference.

Ambivalence about Parochial Jewish Schools

For a group of individuals who have made their homes in culturally diverse neighborhoods where there are often few other Jewish families, it is not surprising that very few DJDS parents talk as though they regard day-school education as a normative option. On the contrary, many parents articulate deep ambivalence about the merits of day-school education in general, and DJDS in particular.

The anxiety expressed by the Lowes about cultural ghettoization, the social mix in the school, and an imbalanced curriculum is shared by others, although, notably, it is expressed most sharply (if not exclusively) by those who themselves attended Jewish day schools as children and who seem haunted by a determination to avoid the worst aspects of their own schooling experiences. This was the case for Michelle and Joe Kleinman, a married couple who had attended the same day school in a small Ontario town until grades 4 and 5 and who for the last two years had lived not far from DJDS in a neighborhood that they described as "family oriented and politically progressive, in terms of race, religion, and sexual orientation." Like the Lowes, they expressed concerns about the social mix in the school (they found it less diverse than people claimed) and about its curriculum ("we don't want God shoved down their throats"), but their ambivalence centered mainly on the political ramifications of their choice.

Michelle: The school was incredibly impressive. I couldn't believe it. It seemed like the most fabulous place. I couldn't imagine something better for my daughter. . . . But we had a huge political problem because we really support the public school system, so it was a big, big dilemma for us whether to support a private school even though I in particular wanted her to have a Jewish education.

Joe: For me it was like a really difficult decision to make. . . . The ideological and political aspects of the decision to send a child to private school weighs down on me. . . . If you pull a kid out of public school you are denying the school that funding. So you are in fact depriving the public school system of money or at least your school of money.

I mean, frankly, if it wasn't a Jewish school she wouldn't be going there; she would be in the public system. I mean we really talked about the *only* justification we felt for sending our child to a private school is that she is going to get a Jewish education, and that's the only justification and that's why we sent her. Otherwise, we don't believe that our child should have those [private school] privileges.

Michelle: One of the ways that we've kind of consoled ourselves about this feeling of abandoning the public system is . . . in terms of the Jewish education. I mean, like, I went until grade 4 and I got quite a substantial Jewish education and Jewish base from that. So we have no intention of Tina continuing any longer than she has to.

The Hillbergs (Mike, who went to day school from grade 2 to grade 6, and Maytal, who grew up on a secular kibbutz in Israel) talk in similar terms about their difficulties in withdrawing from the public school system. In their case, they had returned six months previously from spending two years in Israel where they had taken their children "to ground them in Israel, family, and Hebrew." Maytal admits:

In a way, I'm still grieving about not sending Adina to the [neighborhood] public school because I like it so much, because I believe in the public school system, because I believe in learning in your community.

If we hadn't gone to Israel we wouldn't have come to DJDS. . . . It's not that the school wasn't impressive. My impressions were that it was a good school. It was quite small but I didn't feel connected to the community that it was representing. . . . I feel an

affinity to a nonaffiliated Jewish crowd, and [at DJDS] this is kind
of an organized Jewish crowd. . . . I could not relate to the Jewish,
to the religious component of it, because I grew up very, very secular. And I couldn't get my head around how it would be to abide
by Jewish laws that I grew up not respecting. . . . Academically, I
think our public school is pretty good as well. So Adina would
have probably stayed in the public system. But, having gone to
Israel, she learned Hebrew. It was a shame to let her Hebrew slip,
and that's why—that is the reason for choosing DJDS.

In the case of Carrie and Ian Maybaum, both of whom went to day
school from kindergarten to grade 8, and who live today in what
they characterize as a multiethnic midtown neighborhood, their
ambivalence has fewer political overtones but seems no less conflicted. They make clear:

> Carrie: We never looked for a Jewish school. We both went
> through day schools. I've taught at a day school and have moved
> on. . . . I left [a day-school teaching position] without the best
> taste in my mouth, and at that point there was no way my kids
> were ever going to Jewish day schools. . . . I'm now [in a senior
> position] at an independent French-speaking school, but I was-
> n't too sure I wanted my kids where I work.

Coming from families where some of their siblings' children
attend day school, they explain their ambivalence about day
school in the following terms:

> Carrie: I think the biggest thing for me was I didn't want to end
> up at a Jewish day school just because that's what everybody
> does, or because everybody says it's the right school. So there
> was that resistance. . . . I didn't want to do it because my par-
> ents wanted me to do it. I wanted it to be because we want to
> do it. . . . The other day schools did not interest us at all. . . . We
> are not those kinds of people. It's not the community I would
> feel comfortable with.

They put their son's name down for a nearby public school
for which they were just outside the appropriate district. But, in
Carrie's words, "the decision was made for us, we couldn't get him
in." Under these circumstances, so Ian explains, DJDS seemed

like their next best option, regardless of whether it was a Jewish school.

> Ian: Daniel is going to a Jewish day school because of the DJDS, not because we felt our kid had to go to a Jewish day school. While we were on the fence of, should we do it, should we not do it, the school itself was the reason we chose to do it. As opposed to, it's the best Jewish day school for him. It was the best school for him, that was the decision we made, and it happened to be a Jewish day school.

In some instances, parents do not share the same ambivalence about day-school education. In one case, Harry Funk, a graduate of nine years in day schools, fears that the environment might be too insular and may not sufficiently stimulate his son. He would prefer his children to go to the local public school, but in educational matters he defers to his wife, Dina (also a day-school graduate), who says that she has "known ever since she was a child that when she had children they were going to go to Jewish day school."

In another more unusual case, Michael Fine, a writer who describes himself as feeling very Jewish but not at all religious, never went to day school as a child but experienced a varied Jewish education in supplementary school, summer camp, and Israel. He would prefer his daughters to be in a quality public school because he feels that they (like he did) can develop a robust Jewish identity without being entirely surrounded by Jews. Given that he cannot afford to maintain a car because of the hefty day-school fees he pays, he would very much prefer to be without the financial stress.

Michael's ex-partner, Joanna, whom he never married, has never converted to Judaism (and is herself training to be a public school teacher), but she is determined that "our kids go to school with Jewish kids. There is a lot of anti-Semitism in public schools right now and I hate my kids being exposed to it when I'm not there and I can't protect them." Michael doesn't share what he regards as Dina's oversensitivity but, like her, despairs of the quality of education in the public system "when teachers are poorly equipped to deal with classrooms where there are 17 languages and 23 kids."

Although parents in the other two Toronto day-school samples we interviewed also expressed concerns about the particular institutions they selected, in terms of both social mix (too exclusive) and curriculum (too Jewish), they did not communicate a similar generalized ambivalence about Jewish day-school education that seems, among DJDS parents, to indicate an a priori preference for public education. For example, of the ten families randomly selected for interview at the Ben Gurion School, only two indicated that they seriously considered a nonparochial alternative, most likely French immersion, because as one parent put it, "That's the best that the public system has to offer, sort of the closest thing to private school." At the Rav Kook School, there weren't any families who talked of public school as a possibility. At DJDS, the patterns were reversed, with only two of the sample of fourteen families indicating that they would only have considered a day school. In similar fashion, whereas in the Ben Gurion and Rav Kook samples a number of families planfully chose to live in neighborhoods where they could be close to day schools, for DJDS families the closeness or convenience of day schools was not at all a factor in their housing decision. Most had not imagined that day school would be an option for their children.

The Search for a Quality Education

The fundamental suspicion of day schools articulated by many DJDS parents makes it all the more compelling to ask what ultimately brought families to the school. Given the ambivalence many expressed about day schools in general, one has to wonder what it was about DJDS that so much appealed to them.

A most revealing answer to these questions is provided by the case of Ed and Sharon Manning. Both Ed and Sharon grew up in Toronto. Sharon, whose family was Jewish, attended "alternative schools" for most of her elementary education. Ed, whose family was not Jewish, attended local public schools. The two met and married in Vancouver where they lived for a couple of years. When Sharon became pregnant they moved back to Toronto in order to be closer to family.

On their return, Ed started a plumbing company, and Sharon, who is a qualified elementary school teacher, taught at the Home School, an alternative independent school that she had attended as a child and where she still retained a close connection. That's where their eldest child attended junior kindergarten until the couple who ran the school (and who had been running it since it opened in the 1960s) announced they were retiring. "That's when," Sharon explained, she and Ed "started doing the open house circuit," researching around six different public and private schools.

Their review of the schools they explored (and their detailed assessment of the strengths and weaknesses of those schools) reveals a great deal about what parents consider when they weigh schooling alternatives. Their account also makes explicit what makes DJDS attractive to families who might not otherwise have considered sending their child to a Jewish day school.

Having started out with a child in an alternative private school, one of the first options the Mannings researched was "Live Wire," an alternative public school that was close to where they worked. Unfortunately, they found teachers struggling to manage multi-age classes for children with diverse needs and learning styles. As an alternative school, there was more parent participation, which they liked, but from what they saw "that just meant more brownies or bake sales." The building also "looked like any other run-down public school without any funding."

They explain that they didn't even visit the neighborhood public school just up the street from where they live because, based on "the little bit of interaction [they] had with it, it wasn't acceptable . . . which was unfortunate because [they] love the idea of having [their] children playing with children in [their] neighborhood, and having this sense of community." Regrettably, in Sharon's opinion, "the principal there was just running it completely the wrong way."

They put their names down at the Institute for Child Studies, a university-based laboratory school, because the application was free. But they never heard back.

As far as private school options were concerned, they checked out a few alternatives. The Graham School was one possibility, but knowing both its location in an exclusive neighborhood and the clientele it catered to, it wasn't attractive to the Mannings. As Sharon explained, "It wasn't our priority, since part of [our concern] was finding a community for us as well."

They "did an observation" at Nottingham Academy, a private school close to their home. But, as Sharon puts it, their literacy program made them cringe. They were also put off by the school's traditional ethos: uniforms, standing up, and an agenda for online homework assignments.

It was after exploring so many disappointing alternatives that they came to "check out" DJDS, after having heard about the school at the traditional-egalitarian synagogue they very occasionally attend. Ed clarifies:

> We should say that one of the reasons why we chose to go to the open house at DJDS was just the sheer fact that Sharon's family is Jewish. That's what made it one of our options. It wasn't necessarily the driving force that we wanted or that we had a real expectation of our child having a Jewish education. But you are welcomed to join the program if your family is Jewish, so we thought that's one of our options, let's go check it out.

Given that these don't sound like auspicious reasons for coming to DJDS, it's worth quoting at length how Ed and Sharon describe their reaction after their first visit to the school. In doing so, they give expression to the multiple considerations that school-choice literature frequently notes as determining school quality for parents.

> Ed: So we go to the open house and, we have said it so many times, Joanna, the senior kindergarten teacher was phenomenal. The classroom was very disciplined and challenged, yet the children were made to feel comfortable and welcome to explore ideas and their own individuality without being stifled. As well, the classroom set-up was very nice. This was probably the last open house that we had gone to. Like we had already seen five or six different schools and then we came into this environment. . . . It's a small school and coming in the front door there were people welcoming us, there's an immediate feel that you

get. And the people working in the office: the principal came out and knew who we were as we were coming in, and that sort of thing. It was a very welcoming environment. . . . So, religion aside, it seemed like the most appropriate education that we wanted to give our child.

RS: I'll turn to Sharon: What were your impressions of the open house?

Sharon: Yeah I liked it too. Like Ed came out of there going, oh my God this is it! It definitely had what we were looking for. I mean it had children's art work on the wall. Another thing that I was looking at when I would walk into the other schools, is all these kinds of Scholar's Choice posters that had been stapled up, which I hate. They had kids' art work everywhere and the books were good, there were no readers in the classroom. Everybody seemed really warm for the most part, and even looking at the parents who were at the open house . . .

Ed: They were dressed similar to us.

Sharon: You know they weren't done up, I mean there were definitely done up people at this school, which I was shocked to see, but for the most part people were wearing jeans and T-shirts. It was more like the downtown schlumpy intellectual Jews as opposed to like the Forest Hill crowd, you know like the nanny, cell phone, minivan crowd. . . . I liked the classroom and I liked basically everything that they had to say about it. And like Ed said, we were more looking for a good education than a Jewish education. And actually it was something I wasn't even considering giving my kids. It's ironic my whole family like . . .

Ed: They are all pretty shocked.

Sharon: Yes, they were pretty shocked [laughs]. My cousins are way more religious than I am, and their kids are at Ben Gurion, and my other cousin is a rabbi, but it was never something I would have imagined that I would send my kids to. But then the more Ed liked it, the more I thought about it. I just thought back on my teaching experience. And whenever I had kids who were religious, Jews or non-Jews, they were really like nice kids. They were always the kids who were really thoughtful and kind; more so than other kids, and so I thought, well, so religion isn't such . . . like it can be a good thing in education. Yes, so everybody was pretty shocked that I went there, but happily shocked. My mother was just starting to set the groundwork for taking them every Saturday or Sunday to go to a religious school and all this kind of stuff. Because she wanted them to get a little bit more than what she gave us. So she was really happy.

What makes Sharon and Ed's story so powerful is, first, the way it lends what Van Mannen (1988) calls apparency to the kind of abstract or general claims that are often made about the grounds for school choice. Their account brings particularity to otherwise formal concerns with curriculum, safety, social mix, and convenience. Second, their story makes explicit how carefully and seriously parents can treat the question of where to school their children. The Mannings demonstrate that there really are parents who pay attention to wall displays, reading programs, and the mood of office staff. At the same time, their surprising journey to DJDS makes evident the contingency and unpredictability that runs through the process of making a schooling decision. If the directors at the Home School hadn't retired, Ed and Sharon may not have had to consider any other school options. If Ed had deferred responsibility to Sharon for all aspects of their children's Jewish education, it is highly likely that they would have gone elsewhere. Notably it was he, the non-Jewish partner, who was first captivated by the school and who pressed his wife to try it out.

Where Sharon and Ed differ from many other parents is in the way their school search seemed to be focused on determining what in objective terms constituted the best educational environment. Perhaps this was a consequence of Sharon's background in education, but in contrast to most other parents, they talked little about the particular educational needs of their own children and more about the general merits and faults of the schools they researched. This almost clinical tone is quite different from that employed by others we interviewed who, though no less concerned with educational quality, expressed this concern in relation to the particular needs of their child. Quality, for most other parents, is determined by how well a school can serve an individual child rather than by a set of general merits that will benefit all children.

Thus the kind of qualities that Ed and Sharon found at DJDS and that they talked about in quite general terms have significance for others because they signify an environment that will serve the needs of a particular individual: a "shy child," an adopted child of color with a single mother, a child "who's different from your average five-year-old" and who won't "conform to a mold," one who will otherwise suffer because of a hearing problem in a larger, less nurturing classroom, or one who will feel unsafe as one of the only Jews in the classroom. Choosing a school is, in most cases, not about finding the school that *is* best but about the one that *fits* best.

It is worth emphasizing also that the educational qualities that bring parents such as Ed and Sharon to DJDS do not appeal to all (Jewish) parents. The fact that the school deemphasizes competition, that it "emphasizes the individuality of students," and that the arts are integrated throughout the curriculum are taken by parents at other schools as evidence of a lack of seriousness or rigor, as being "hokey," in the words of one mother. By way of contrast, when Ben Gurion parents talk about the educational qualities that attracted them to their children's school, they employ a profoundly different educational language: they celebrate the fact that "the children are pushed," that they're "challenged," and that the school promises and has a long track record of delivering "academic excellence." They are attracted to the school by the professionalism and efficiency of the preschool faculty they meet at gatherings for prospective parents. This differs markedly from how DJDS parents perceive the nurturing they witness in the kindergarten classroom and the pioneering spirit they sense in the school, which is so much different from the "altogether too smooth operation" at Ben Gurion. If parents are attracted by certain qualities at the school, these are not of a generic nature.

Concern about Children's Jewishness

Earlier studies of liberal Jewish day schools found that many parents were attracted to these institutions in spite of their Jewishness (Kelman 1984; Zeldin 1988). It was suggested that these schools appealed to liberal Jews because they offered a cheap version of private education (with the promise of small class sizes and a selective population), without suffering from the problematic elitism that accompanies nonsectarian private education. According to this argument, if schools offered a good enough general education, parents (and children) would be prepared to tolerate the many hours devoted to the Hebrew and Jewish studies curriculum.

It is perhaps tempting to think of DJDS parents in these terms, particularly in light of their general ambivalence concerning Jewish day schools and their talk of finding DJDS in their search for the right school, and not necessarily a Jewish one. How else can one interpret comments such as that made by the Maybaums that "it wasn't really [their] intent to find a Jewish school," or as the Mannings put it, that "we were more looking for a good education than a Jewish education"?

Our conversations reveal that, in fact, the school's Jewish orientation is of no small significance to many DJDS parents and that this significance is manifest in two discrete ways: in one respect, the school's religious pluralism and egalitarianism mean that some parents are *not* put off the school as they are by other Jewish day schools. At the same time, the school's particular curriculum orientation is genuinely appealing to others who are anxious to provide their children with a knowledge and appreciation for Jewish culture and life. The first reaction is a corollary of the ambivalence parents express about day schools in general. It sees expression in parents' surprise that the school "is open-minded about the different levels of Judaism practiced in people's homes, that it is open-minded about conceptions and beliefs in God, it's open-minded about sexual orientation." These characteristics are especially attractive to parents who, in their own self-descriptions, "have mixed feelings about Israel," "don't know how much you have to believe in God to be a Jew," "have problems with organized religion," and are connected with few other institutions in the Jewish community. These parents are genuinely astonished that they can feel comfortable in a formal Jewish educational institution. For those who went to Jewish day schools themselves, and who experienced certain ideas "being rammed down their throats" and were told "this is what they were supposed to do," there is great appeal to a school that "shows respect for each person's Jewish practices."

Analogous to this kind of double-negative perspective (where the school is attractive because it is not doctrinaire or intolerant) were the responses of a small number of parents for whom one of the attractions of the school was that, because it provided Jewish education during the course of the normal work day, children did not have to attend supplementary Jewish school during evenings or weekends. This meant that families were free to go skiing in the winter or simply didn't have to experience the stress of scheduling Hebrew school on top of numerous other after-school commitments.

It would be misleading, however, to conclude that most parents think about the school's Jewishness in these lukewarm terms. Contrary to our own expectations, we found families who were drawn to the school because of a deep interest in providing their children with a Jewish education. In a few powerful cases, this was inspired by their sense that, as a conversionary or single-parent family, they lacked the resources to provide their children with an adequate sense of what it means to be Jewish. As one mother put it, "The school can give Jasmine the Jewishness that I want to give, but that I don't think I could." In other instances this interest in Jewish education came from parents' thoughtful determination to enable their children to make what they called "informed choices" about their Jewish lives when they are older.

One of the most powerful statements of these concerns came from Ruth Goldman, a single mother with an adopted daughter of color whom she had brought to Canada. Ruth had grown up in what she called a traditional Conservative Jewish family, from which "in many respects she regarded [herself] as a refugee." After her father had died and she had been responsible for organizing the appropriate mourning rituals, she came to realize, she says, "how much I knew [about Judaism] through living it and through osmosis and everything. I realized that I wanted my daughter to know. I thought that to be secular was horrible. . . . Cultural ignorance is really dangerous and very sad." Ruth came to the school "driven by [her] fear of her [daughter's] ignorance, that she would end up a completely secular Jew, and not be grounded. I wanted her to be grounded. . . . I wanted her to know how to doven [pray]" but in an atmosphere of gender equity. "Gender equity is fundamental. I can't get my head around a practice of Judaism . . . that would treat her unequally. I mean I brought her to Canada so that she wouldn't be a second class person. I come from a generation where the Jewish God was an old man saying no. I wanted everything Jewish that Erica does to be joyous. . . . So there was only really one school."

This determination to provide one's children with the Jewish resources they might otherwise never access is also exemplified in the case of Barb and John Spencer, a couple who live farther from the school than almost any other family, in a neighborhood where there are few other Jewish families. They offer a similar sort of rationale for choosing the school, but as Barb explains, they were also influenced by other considerations:

> I converted and John is traditional in his observance but he is not at all religious. So we don't have a really religious home, but we wanted to expose our children to a Jewish community and have them comfortable with that. So I think that was part of the reason why we wanted to be at a Jewish day school. But we were looking for a place where we would fit in, where I wouldn't feel uncomfortable because I converted, that there were more couples like us.

They report that they "went back and forth between public and Jewish day school." They had concerns about public school especially in relation to student-teacher ratios and other quality issues, but most decisive was their anxiety about the consequences of "trying to sneak in a couple of hours on a Sunday to remind the kids that they're Jewish," as would be the case if they went the public school route. From their perspective, even though there is a daily commute of some forty-five minutes in each direction to DJDS, "going to a Jewish school serves [them] better," because their children would otherwise struggle to develop a sense of Jewish community. John's family live out of town in western Canada, Barb's aren't Jewish, and there's hardly any Jewish community where Barb and John live. As John puts it, "Here there is nothing other than us to support what Nina learns in school."

For another conversionary family, the Wagners, the school was attractive for different reasons. Although they had been put off public school by their child's experience in kindergarten—"The economics are such that the teachers have so few resources that if they can stop the kids killing each other, they're doing a really good job"—they nevertheless thought very seriously about a French immersion option, even placing their child on the registration list. Ultimately they decided that "it was more important to have a Jewish education than to be fluent in French" and that Gary, their son, is "no longer bifurcated between what he does [at home], what he does at shul and what he does at school." Brian (who converted to Judaism after they married) describes the family as being traditional Conservatives: "I don't work on Shabbat or *Yomtov*. We keep kosher; we go to shul; it's a Jewish home; there are also Jewish books; and Gary has been nourished on Jewish stories since he was a babe."

Despite their engaged Jewish lifestyle, they preferred not to send their children to the day school in the Conservative synagogue they attend every week, because, as Anne elucidates, it was too insular:

> Everybody goes to the same place. The school and your entire life is around this one building. . . . I think it gives a very insular view of the Jewish community. So when you see people who don't do it exactly this way, you go, oh, what's up, they're not Jewish. . . . I think I just wanted Gary to have a broader view of what the Jewish community is. That it's not just the way we do things. There is a whole range of how to be Jewish and it doesn't just involve going to Emet Veyatziv [their synagogue].

Brian elaborates further on why they felt comfortable being among the small minority of highly observant families at DJDS: "What I like about what DJDS brings is its diversity. . . . It makes it possible for someone [like me] who observes kashrut, and who observes Shabbat, to participate. And it's accepted at some level as a normative expression of Judaism without excluding the other range of expressions. So I like it because it's within a Halachic framework but not one that makes a gold standard of it."

It would be misleading to conclude on the basis of these statements that all (or even most) of the new families at DJDS place their Jewish aspirations ahead of all other considerations when choosing a school, unlike many of those at Ben Gurion and unlike the great majority of those at Rav Kook. At Rav Kook it was not unusual for parents to say that although they "knew" that they could get a better education elsewhere, they chose this school because it "fit best" with their religious practices at home. DJDS parents indicate a different set of priorities, but there is still no question that, despite (and perhaps because of) their tenuous connection to other forms of formal Jewish engagement, they do take serious account of their children's Jewish needs when selecting the school. Nowhere is this seen more vividly than in the case of the Kleinmans who, as previously discussed, were terribly conflicted about abandoning the public school system for DJDS. Joe Kleinman makes clear what for him tipped the balance in favor of the school:

> I always considered myself Jewish but it wasn't a prominent part of my life. But you see your kids get to the point where their cognitive development is such that you know that this is the time to offer Judaism to your child and you have to ask yourself how important is it to you. And I decided at that point that this was important enough to me to reintegrate Judaism in to my life to send her to a Jewish school. That was a big part of the decision for me.

In a later chapter we see that the stresses created by a decision such as this can have challenging ramifications for parents, teachers, and children. For the moment it will do to note an easily missed dimension to Joe's response that points to a final decisive element in paving the road to DJDS. To repeat Joe's rationale: "I decided at that point that this was important enough to *me* to reintegrate Judaism in to *my* life to send *her* to Jewish school." As his words indicate, choosing a school for one's child is closely interrelated to making choices about one's own adult life as a Jew.

Anxiety about Belonging and Difference

We have quoted at length from interviews with parents to convey the rich array of considerations they weighed when choosing schools and to indicate what special contextual factors influenced and informed their decisions. Confirmation for the themes that emerge from this qualitative data is provided by a recent multi-city quantitative study conducted by Cohen and Kelner (2007).

Using survey data collected from more than three thousand
respondents, they isolated three determinant attitudes that influence why parents choose (or do not choose) day schools:

1. Aspirations for one's children's Jewish growth.
2. Perceived effectiveness of day schools in producing impact
   in terms of both Jewish identity and academic achievement.
3. And, as an obstacle, the perception that day schools in
   effect ghettoize their students, both by depriving them of
   the ability to interact with non-Jews and by making them
   "too religious."

Cohen and Kelner's findings provide useful confirmation that the
three themes we saw intersecting earlier are at the heart of any
decision to choose a day school. A drawback of their model is that
it does not account for one further concern that emerged in our
interviews as a significant consideration for parents. This, as inti-
mated earlier, concerns the extent to which parents feel that
the school satisfies their own sense of belonging and difference
or, to put it differently, the extent to which it satisfies some of
their own adult concerns. As was suggested in a previous chapter,
although it is somewhat counterintuitive to propose that parents
choose schools for their children on the basis of how well the
schools meet their own needs as adults, we have found that, since
the early days of our inquiry at DJDS, school choice and parents'
subsequent relationship with schools are not merely driven by
concerns about children.

The first time we became aware of such concerns was when we
were observing a mid-September event for new parents and their
"buddies," those parents with whom they were matched when
they first joined the school. This event, advertised as "DJDS New
Family: Orientation and Shmoozefest!!!" was billed as "a great
opportunity to get all those questions answered." It met these
expectations and more when at the start of the evening the principal suggested that, before the formal proceedings start, we go
around the room and allow everyone a chance to say a few words
about themselves and how they came to the school. The principal's intent was to give people an opportunity to break the ice, but

as people began to talk with intensity and a good deal of emotion about their relationship to the school, the meeting assumed an unexpected confessional quality.

Because this event occurred soon after the start of our work in the school, and before we started to interview families in their own homes, we did not feel bold enough to run a tape recorder during the proceedings. In our comments here, we have therefore relied on field notes composed immediately after the event (in the car and at home). Before considering the substance of what was shared at this event, it is important to recognize that the public nature of the setting probably constrained some of what people shared, introducing a quality of "faithfulness" into what they wanted to be seen as saying. It is worth keeping in mind also that those who attended this event in the role of "buddies" did not constitute a random sample of DJDS families. They were the school's most committed parents who had volunteered (or had been invited) to mentor new members of the community.

Even when taking these constraints into account, the group's comments confirm that people choose (Jewish) schools for a dazzling array of reasons, many of which have been described at greater length earlier. Thus one parent, having sent her child to the unaffiliated Jewish nursery in the same building shared by the school, viewed DJDS as a "natural" choice. Another parent was attracted to a small school for a child with special academic needs. A number of families were drawn to the school because of certain features in the curriculum: its emphasis on the arts, its creativity, its integrative approach to teaching Judaism, or, to put it simply, its quality. As one parent put it with great pithiness, she was looking for a school that was as much as possible like camp. As one might have expected, in all of these instances, the school appealed to parents because of what it offered their children in academic, social, or spiritual terms.

If these constitute conventional expressions of how parents think about their children's schools, a number of other comments confirm that additional factors, deriving from parents' own particular identities and needs, play a role in how they think about their children's schooling. Thus one couple explained how important it was to them that this was a school where other parents also had children late in life. Another couple indicated that they were drawn to being at a school with families who shared their values (e.g., making charitable donations rather than buying gifts for friends' birthdays) and who dressed like them (enabling them to attend school meetings in cycle gear). For one parent, the Jewish partner in an interfaith marriage, it was important to give her child and herself a Jewish connection. In these instances parents indicate that their attachment to the school is related to the ways in which they construct their own identities as adults. To this extent, the school offers them and their children what Merz and Furman (1997, 14, following Tönnies 1963) call communities of kinship, neighborhood, and mind. The school fits with who they are.

Some of those who spoke went still further in describing the significance of the school in their lives. In fact, it may have been because these people talked in such personal terms that the mood of the session became so charged. For one parent, joining the school was "a kind of coming home"; for another, it was "a second chance" after having had such a miserable experience with Jewish education "the first time," that is, when he went to school as a child. For this parent, involvement at DJDS was a way of "reconnecting to [his] Jewish roots," and it is why he became active in the school even before his children were of school age. One parent spoke for many: when commenting on the school's importance to him and his family, he said, "I'm not sure if it's about what my child gets or what I get."

In a setting such as this where people were, in effect, being asked to declare a public commitment to the school, it was difficult to determine what exactly parents "get" from the school (although the intimacy and intensity of this event testifies to some of the school's appeal). At the very least, however, the general impression left by what parents said alerted us to the significance that the school might hold in their own lives and encouraged us to probe this theme further in our conversations with them when we met in their homes.

As we discussed earlier, even when parents talk about the educational qualities or Jewish character of the school, their comments are interwoven with concern about how comfortable they as adults feel in this setting. As Karen Lowe put it after listing the educational merits of the school that so much appealed to her, "I suspect, like everyone else, you are all looking for somewhere to belong." For intermarried or conversionary families (who constitute seven of the fourteen families who joined DJDS in 2003), this is no small matter when there is such a disjunction between their own experience of schooling and that experienced by their children. For intermarried families there is anxiety about how a non-Jewish partner will be viewed within the school community. For conversionary couples, where both partners are now Jewish, there is still great concern about the cultural deficits that may impede their interactions with others.

Parents repeatedly make explicit that one of the great attractions at DJDS is their perception of it as a place where, as Carrie Maybaum put it, "people [by which she meant both parents and children] don't have to fit a mold." This contrasts with their experiences in other Jewish institutions, such as synagogues and preschools, where, as some report, they "weren't accepted as a Jewish family," either because one partner is not Jewish or because both parents are gay. According to Dina Funk, the school "is so accepting of everything, you know, whether it's a mixed marriage, whether it's a gay couple, whether it's poor, whether it's wealthy. You know, artsy, intellectual. Like it really doesn't matter. You want to send your kids for a Jewish education, you want to be part of this community, then, welcome."

This perception of openness strongly informs parents' expectations of how their children will be treated in the classroom, but it also colors parents' expectations of the reception they themselves will receive and the extent to which they will feel comfortable in the company of other parents. For some, more conventionally, a feeling of comfort and belonging comes from knowing "that there are other couples like us," "people who dress similar to us"— other intellectual types, artists, older couples, or mixed-faith families. But for other parents, comfort derives from knowing that they will be accepted as different and that others won't think them "weird" or unusual for being poor, observant, wealthy, deaf, non-Jewish, or gay. Paradoxically, for these parents a sense of belonging comes from knowing that they can be (and are encouraged to be) different from other families.

These impulses, one indicative of a more conventional search for belonging and fellowship, the other closer to what Shields (2000) calls the search for "a community of difference," are vividly captured by two metaphors offered unprompted by two of our interviewees. Maytal Hillberg, the only parent to have spent most of her life in Israel, likened the school to "a little island of Judaism in the city's downtown." She thereby emphasized what people share when they join the school and how that distinguishes them from much of the world outside. Security and succor come from finding others like themselves. The school is a rare place where those accustomed to spending their lives as a (Jewish) minority taste the experience of being in the majority.

Another parent, Ruth Goldman, paradoxically coming to the school with a much more traditional Jewish orientation, compared the school to "a bouquet of flowers" where, she elaborated, "everyone is not the same, and where difference is good and does not have to be conquered." The school, in these terms, is not so unlike the world outside—it shares something of its diversity. But because of its mission and vision, it also protects and affirms the possibilities of difference.

After spending at least an hour and sometimes much longer in conversation with each of the families we interviewed, our sense is that it is this second impulse that is the more powerful for those who have chosen to join the school. When all parents were asked how similar or different they thought their reasons were for coming to the school from those of other families, there were hardly any who believed that there were many other parents like them. They took the diversity of the parent body for granted and celebrated it. They value the school as a place where they can belong without having to conform. They see it as a venue that can satisfy their needs (those of both their children and themselves) and where they might stretch and grow. What this means is not apparent at the moment of their first encounter with the school. Their focus at that time is on finding the best possible educational environment for their children. Quickly, however, they uncover layers of significance in their choice that point to other potential outcomes.

Choosing a school, and being a parent of a school-age child, is, as Ian Maybaum confessed, a lot more significant than he ever imagined:

> I'm pleasantly surprised by how much I like to talk about [my child's school]. I never thought it would be something like that. . . . You know, you send your child to school, that's what you do. It's part of being a parent. But it's more than that, and I realize that [now], and I definitely did not realize that before. . . . I didn't think as a parent it would be any different [from when I was student], but it does feel different. It's more important.

This last quotation serves as a sharp caution against the tendency to interpret the turn of liberal Jewish families to day schools as flight from a decaying public system or as an indicator of surging Jewish particularism. As we have seen, even those most despondent about public education do not run directly toward a parochial school option. Similarly, some who are unsure about their own Judaism and are highly committed to public schooling may nevertheless find themselves drawn toward day schools of a certain kind. For the parents in our samples, choosing a school is not a matter they take lightly in terms of what is most convenient or most fashionable. It is about as serious as parenting gets, and as we see in the next chapters, it sets in motion a series of processes that have ongoing significance in parents' lives.

What Are Parents Doing at School?

FRAMING THE INTERACTIONS BETWEEN PARENTS AND THEIR CHILDREN'S SCHOOLS

Researching Parent Involvement

The ambivalence, investment, and anxiety that parents display before selecting DJDS for their children is no less evident in their involvements with the school after their children are enrolled. It is to these involvements, their meaning, and their multiple consequences that we now turn, as these provide the most conspicuous starting point for an examination of the relationship between parents and any school that educates their children.

Over the last twenty years, the causes, content, and consequences of parent involvement within schools have been studied from a variety of angles. The causes of parental involvements (and the constraints on them) have been investigated through the prism of numerous academic disciplines. Some, for example, have used political theory and constructs of power, authority, and control to examine the troubled relationships between schools and families in urban settings (Fine 1993; Sarason 1990). Others have turned to psychological theory—in relation, for instance, to parents' role construction, their sense of efficacy, and their perception of whether their child wants them to be involved—to explain why parents become involved in their children's education (Hoover-Dempsey and Sandler 1997). A number of studies have explored the relationship of econometric variables (such as income, employment, and wealth) to aspects of parental involvement (Lareau 2000). The discipline of sociology has been used to account for the role of cultural and social capital in families and of school organizational structure as forces that shape parent involvement (Coleman 1994; Smrekar 1996). Finally, there has been a turn to anthropology to make sense of the problematic interactions between parents and teachers in relation to gender, culture, and language (Delpit 1993; Hargreaves 1999).

The content of parent involvement—the different forms that involvement can take—has been comprehensively explored as well. This has resulted in a detailed typology of what Epstein calls the six major types of partnership activities between school, family, and community (1994). These include (1) basic obligations of parents to establish home environments that support children as students; (2) basic obligations of schools to communicate about school programs and children's progress; (3) parent volunteer roles that support school functions and activities; (4) family involvement in learning and enrichment activities at home that support learning at school; (5) parent participation in decision making, leadership, and advocacy; and (6) school collaboration with the community to integrate resources and services that support students and their families (Epstein 1994; Epstein and Sanders 2000). A basic assumption behind Epstein's typology is that different outcomes are linked to different types of involvement: "Some activities will affect students' skills and scores" in particular subject areas while "other activities are more likely to influence attendance, attitudes, families' confidence about parenting or teachers' respect for families" (Epstein and Sanders 2000, 289). The problem, as Epstein indicates, is that the educational consequences produced by different types of involvement have not been well established. As she cautions, "Research at all grade levels is needed on the effects of specific partnership activities on the attitudes, behaviors and skills of students, parents, and schools" (2000, 296).

In the absence of such research, it is remarkable how extensive has been the examination of the general consequences of parent involvement for children's learning, especially over the last few decades as attempts to increase parent involvement in schooling have become a commonplace feature of educational policy all over the world. Mattingly et al. (2002) identified 213 studies published since 1960 that purported to examine interventions in U.S. public schools aimed at enhancing the impact of parent involvement on children's learning. Their review of such studies (many of which, they found, lacked adequate information about either the intervention concerned or the evaluation methods employed) led them to conclude that there is, in fact, a large gap between popular support for such programs and scientific evidence that confirms their positive impact.

Points of Continuity between School Choice and Involvement

When so much has been written about parental involvement in schools, and when, despite Mattingly et al.'s reservations, it is widely accepted that involving parents in children's education can significantly improve their learning (Hargreaves 1999), what is there to be learned from the case of DJDS that isn't already known?

We suggest that a different and deeper appreciation of the causes and consequences of parent involvement emerges if we probe the points of continuity between the multiple concerns that inform parents' choice of school (as detailed in the previous chapter) and the way parents relate to the school once their children are enrolled. That is to say, we suggest looking at parent involvement not only in terms of what it contributes to the quality of student learning (the predominant focus in the literature cited earlier) but also in relation to elements of meaning and significance in parents' own lives, particularly, in our case, the elements reflected in and activated by the behaviors and intentions of Jewish parents engaged in the act of choosing a Jewish school for their children.

This orientation points to two assumptions. The first is that school choice is an active construct in parents' ongoing interactions with schools. This assumes that parents who choose their children's schools will relate to these schools in ways shaped by the reasoning and circumstances behind their choices, even if, as previous studies of parent involvement in schools of choice have shown, the particular trajectory created by the act of choice may tend in more than one direction. Thus, on the one hand, we can expect, as Smrekar and Goldring (1999) report, that the sources and dynamics of school choice will create the conditions and processes that lead to basic elements of community. Parents will develop a sense of fellowship, shared interest, and mutual goals with other families who have made similar school choices (Smrekar 1996). Having chosen a school, they will seek opportunities to make the best of their selection and will work with the (professional and lay) partners in their children's education (Bryk, Lee, and Holland 1993). On the other hand, as critics of school choice have suggested, we can also anticipate a different dynamic. From this perspective, school choice is itself an extreme product of the individualistic pursuit of personal goals and will therefore be unlikely to result in parents' developing a sense of fellowship or community with other "consumers" who may happen to have made the same choices. It is likely that once parents have made an initial choice of school, they will delegate responsibility to the school for their children's education, exempting their own involvement (Bauch 1989). It is our assumption that whichever trajectory of involvement has developed at DJDS, the extent and shape of these trajectories will be related in some way to the original act of choice.

The second assumption behind our research focus derives from what we found to be influential in shaping parents' school choice in the first place: that parents' interactions with their children's Jewish schools are not exclusively concerned with the quality of children's learning. Thus we assume that just as Jewish school choice was itself informed by a range of interests and needs in parents' own lives (such as their search for Jewish community or for Jewish cultural resources absent in their homes), so might their ongoing interactions with schools shape and be shaped by a similar range of concerns.

As was the case with our study of routes to school enrollment, here too we turn to the ethnographic tools of interview and observation in order to uncover what parents value and find meaningful. This does not mean that we expect to identify modes of parental involvement not previously described by others. Rather we turn to familiar modes of parent-school interaction (such as volunteering in class, sitting on committees, helping with schoolwork at home) to see whether these involvements are motivated by concerns already visible in the process of choosing the school and whether these involvements have meaning and consequence for parents.

Reframing Involvement

A brief example will indicate what this orientation reveals. In private Jewish day schools such as DJDS, a significant number of parents sit on committees that govern and guide the school. As we have seen, for conventional research in the sociology of education, involvements such as these demand attention in terms of how they ultimately improve the quality of the learning environment for children. But from our perspective, concerned as we are with the potential significance of such involvements for parents, it is important to identify the motivations with which parents join school committees and what in turn their participation might mean in their own lives. Thus at DJDS we have found it important to distinguish between parent participants who join the Religion and Educational Policy Committee so as to advance a single issue that particularly weighs on their children (say, how much homework they must do every night) and other parents who may no longer have children in the school but remain deeply committed to the school's vitality as a community institution with which they feel a profound sense of connection. We compare these parents, in turn, with those who are involved because of their commitment to a set of ideas and practices that they think all in the school should support, and other committee members who are inspired to participate because they enjoy interactions with other Jewish adults and find that committee work provokes them to think deeply about their own values and commitments.

It is our thesis that such differences in motivation have important consequences in terms of the significance of the school in parents' lives. More immediately, awareness of these differences also helps explain the sometimes paradoxical, sometimes contradictory messages we encountered at DJDS regarding the intensity of parent involvement at the school.

As was mentioned in the introduction, one of the reasons we first became interested in DJDS was because of our sense of the school as a place where parents were present with remarkable frequency and intensity. This was an impression reinforced by interviews with teachers and parents. And yet the more time we spent in the school, the more we also heard complaints, in interviews and in casual conversations, about parent apathy or about the difficulty of getting parents to volunteer. At times it seemed as if we were being told about two parent bodies; indeed, frequently that was how this apparent inconsistency was explained to us. Although the school was only five years old, we were told that there was a generation of pioneering and highly involved families who in their level of engagement and their Jewish and educational values were different from a new generation of more apathetic parents who were seen more as consumers than creators in the school. This dichotomy—to which many of the "older" interviewees subscribed—did not in fact match the reality we uncovered in our interviews with teachers and with parents: we found that there were both new and old parents who were involved and also those who were apathetic.

No less paradoxical, our interviews with parents revealed that though a vocal minority of parents were highly critical of the school for one reason or another, those who were most critical were not necessarily the ones who withdrew their children. In other words, there was no clear correlation between satisfaction with the quality of education in the school and ongoing enrollment.

In this chapter we see that these confusing messages reflect the multiple and frequently selective ways in which parents relate to the school and also important differences in why they become involved. These patterns are paradoxical only if parent involvement is viewed as being concerned exclusively or even primarily with children's development and learning—in other words, if it is viewed through a singular interpretative frame that captures just one part of the reality of parent-school interaction. If, however, the relationship between parents and school is viewed through a series of different frames, each concerned with different outcomes and purposes, not only does this confusion dissipate, but also causes and consequences of parent-school interactions come into view that would be otherwise overlooked.

This strategy of "reframing," or re-viewing a confusing organizational situation in relation to discrete foci or frames, is an intellectual approach that Bolman and Deal have employed with great effect in their effort to decode organizational complexity (2003). In their words, to see the same organization simultaneously from multiple perspectives, and to think about the same thing in more than one way, can be a powerful tool for gaining clarity (18–19). We take up the four frames Bolman and Deal use for the study of organizations—the human resource (concerned with the needs of individuals in an organization), the structural (concerned with organizational efficiency), the political (where members of an organization compete for power), and the symbolic (where members find meaning and inspiration)—so as to separate out the different purposes with which parents interact with the school, the different roles they play in these interactions, and the different consequences of these interactions. As we found when employing this strategy in a preliminary fashion in a parallel study (Pomson 2007), this multiperspectival approach reinvigorates the notion of parent involvement by making visible its multidimensional causes and consequences.

The Human-Resource Frame: Parents as Partners Helping Their Children in/with School

Without doubt, the most common impulse behind parental involvement at DJDS is parents' desire to have influence over their own children's learning and development. This, it seems, is the corollary of parents' deliberately selecting the school, often after a lengthy period of consideration and comparison.

At first glance this impulse seems like an acute expression of parents' wanting to make the best of their investment or of wanting "to get value," as one parent put it, having chosen to pay more than ten thousand dollars a year for their child's schooling. It is a phenomenon another parent (talking about others rather than herself) described more caustically: "I think a lot of parents expect that because they're sending their kids to a private school, the school should be able to tailor-make a program for their child. . . . So they end up checking every single thing their child does, and looking over their child's shoulder and the teacher's shoulder all the time" (John Richards).

While this feeling of entitlement corresponds to a phenomenon Smrekar found in a (1996) study of parents at a private Catholic elementary school, we saw little of it at DJDS. Only one family talked about their own motivations in this way, although quite a few did attribute such motivations to others. Teachers did occasionally complain about parents who "seem to think that their child is entitled to an individualized program," but parents and teachers generally agreed that although there is an acute level of parent interest at DJDS in "how one's child is doing," this interest comes less from wanting to get value for money and more from other sources: from parents coming to the school with high (some say unrealistic) expectations for their children, from parents being committed to sophisticated (some say utopian) educational ideals concerning what the school should be offering, or simply from parents feeling that it is important to be highly involved in their children's day-to-day lives (an intensifying phenomenon that scholars and journalists have noted in a number of private-school settings [Gibbs 2005; Keyes 2005]).

The problem for teachers (and ethnographers) is that it is difficult to distinguish between these different sources of involvement, because all see expression in heightened parental sensitivity to what children are doing in school and also in a generally high level of interaction between parents and teachers. It is no wonder that under these circumstances even highly competent teachers complain of experiencing a lack of trust when they find themselves having to spend what one teacher-interviewee called "an alarming amount of time" on communication with parents, phone calls, e-mails, and meetings with parents above and beyond conferences and report cards. This same teacher admitted that "sometimes I kind of want to say, just let me do my job, you know."

Yet, as another teacher reveals when asked to provide some examples of what parents want most to talk to her about, parents don't seem to be exhibiting distrust or an exaggerated sense of entitlement:

AP: What do parents generally make contact about?

PT: It could be good things [i.e., sharing good news], that Suzie hadn't being doing a lot of cursive at home. You've been doing it in class, and now we find that her cursive is amazing . . . or we just want you to know that we got our six times table over the weekend, or my son went away on a trip and he visited another classroom and stood up in front of the class and talked about what it means to be Jewish.

Then there is the flip side, the things that are negative things. My child is having trouble at recess, maybe you can keep an eye out for his interactions with this other child. Or we are just not getting the rocks and minerals concept, can you go over that?

Perhaps it is surprising that parents should think it necessary to communicate about all of these matters (particularly when parents seek to share such information at all times of day, even after class has started in the morning). But these communications attest more fundamentally to a desire to knit home and school closer together, to a view of parents and teachers sharing in a joint endeavor, and to parental investment in their children and their lives at home and school.

At DJDS we were told often (again, usually by people talking about others rather than themselves) that this heightened level of interest had something to do with the relative age of the parent body: "You get a whole section of older parents, parents who have their one and only kid in their forties, and parents like that tend to be very involved; actually 'involved' is a nice way of putting it." This explanation (one that has taken hold as one of the school's founding myths because of the disproportionate presence of older parents among the first families) doesn't, however, really account for the investment shown by the majority of families in the school, most of whom are neither older parents nor one-child families.

As suggested earlier, it is more likely that parents' deep interest and involvement in their children's schooling is tied to the strong educational convictions that inspired them to choose DJDS in the first place and that continue to stimulate their relationship with the school. As we saw in the previous chapter, most parents selected the school not because it satisfied a generic set of criteria that might easily be found in other schools but rather because they saw DJDS as an educational institution with a particular identity that fit well with the kinds of downtown values to which they themselves were committed. It is because of their commitment to these values that they pay careful attention to what happens in their child's classroom. They want to be sure that the school does indeed cultivate the diversity, religious pluralism, commitment to social action, intellectual inquiry, and arts-based education they sought and expected. Their heightened concern does not indicate a lack of trust or an exaggerated sense of entitlement, as might be assumed from some of the earlier comments, but rather a commitment to a deep set of convictions that are focused on their child.

These commitments see the most proactive expression in parents' frequent efforts to bring to teachers' attention opportunities and resources that they believe will appropriately enrich their child's educational experience. In the background here is a sense expressed by many parents that although the core faculty at DJDS are highly competent (even excellent) pedagogues, the cultural world of the teachers differs from that of most of the families. Parents have a strong sense of themselves as "downtown" people and of the downtown area offering a range of resources and opportunities that might enrich their child's education. They feel that because almost all of the teachers come from uptown (and, as one parent complained, don't even know their way around the city on public transit), the parents have "to work on the teachers" to ensure that their children will receive the kind of "progressive" education they desire.

This dynamic is exemplified by the case of Jack and Joyce Lewis, both of whom work in cultural institutions downtown and who were originally attracted to DJDS because of what they identified as its commitment to the arts, social action, and religious pluralism. Joyce explains that although she is ready to pitch in when the school calls for volunteers, for example, on pizza days or fairs, "because that way she gets to see her kids in context," she is not enthralled with "parents' being cast in the role of muffin makers and bake sale people." Instead she finds she can be involved "on a more meaningful level . . . by taking advantage of her connections in downtown institutions so as to enrich the children's experience." "Normally a school group wouldn't get a curator to talk to them. They would call someone out of the education department to take them around, give them the same tour that everybody gets, which is often fine and good. But having the curator . . . talk to the kids can sometimes generate insights for them that they might not get. So having a connection is one way of enriching their experience." Jack elaborates on the same theme, providing further examples of how, with "pushing from parents," teachers were persuaded to take the children to different exhibits downtown, on unusual field trips, or to arts performances involving DJDS parents. In a similar vein, Tom, another father, describes his child's teacher being persuaded to take the class to a particular concert "because we marched in and I handed them the flyer." These examples constitute some of the strongest expressions of parent involvement as it occurs within a "human resources" frame: it is initiated by parents, it is focused on their own child, but while directed at their own child it also provides benefits to other children and to the school community.

The Structural Frame: Parents as Volunteers, Helping Make Their Children's School More Effective

The great challenge for faculty and for lay leadership is that while parents display an almost inexhaustible capacity for involvement when their own children take part, it becomes harder to recruit them as volunteers for projects focused on the school as a whole. This is a mode of involvement that constitutes what Bolman and Deal (2003) call the structural frame. It is where involvement is largely initiated by teachers or administrators, where it is focused on the school as an organization, and where it is assumed that what benefits the whole school will also benefit the children of those who volunteer.

How much of a problem it is to stimulate parental involvement within this frame is a matter of perspective. On the one hand, DJDS, like other cash-strapped private schools, operates a great number of parent committees that facilitate the school's operation. Parents serve on the eleven committees of the school's board and on the thirteen committees operated by the parents' association, and in addition they support numerous ad-hoc initiatives. On the one hand, given its small size, the school seems well served by volunteers who take on the same array of responsibilities that would be demanded of a larger parent body by a larger institution. On the other hand, activist parents complain that the school struggles to find volunteers to run whole-school programs such as the school picnic, the Friday challah program, and the book fair. They protest that the school seems to depend on the same small number of people for many of these events.

Some parents are convinced of a decline in volunteerism and see it as evidence of a shift in school culture as DJDS has matured from being more or less parent run (as was the case in its first couple of years) to being led and managed by professionals who, it is claimed, prefer to keep parents at arm's length. They suggest that newer parents tend to rely on paid professionals to take care of matters—such as lunchtime activities or special classroom events—that were once managed by volunteers.

There are a few intimations of this shift. For example, some of the founding parents talk about their original involvement with the school in an unusually cerebral fashion. They talk of their commitment to the school as an abstract idea, which strictly speaking was all the school was when they first became involved. Ray Lombard, a founding member of the board, describes his original involvement in the following terms: "They [the school's founders] were looking for volunteers, and I wasn't working at the time. I wanted to work on the school because it sounded really interesting, not at all knowing that I was interested in my kids going there." Of course, Ray knew that one day his own children would need to go to school somewhere, but it seems that at the start he was attracted to the notions of building a school from scratch and of trying to realize a highly idealized educational vision for the downtown community without immediate application to his own children.

This same institutional idealism sees expression on those occasions when parents initiate projects in the school for purposes that go beyond the immediate needs of their own children. A vivid example of this is provided by two parents who took it upon themselves to introduce a recycling program to the school when the faculty moved slowly to introduce such a program. As one of these parents explained: "If you have a school that has the kind of character that we would expect, then surely the majority of people should have [recycling] as a priority. We knew the faculty were extremely busy [too busy to take on this program], so we were prepared. We brought [the boxes to recycle] in. We were prepared to make it as simple as possible to have kids rotate to take the stuff home" (Adele Wallace).

This intervention has a different quality from that initiated by another group of parents who describe how they "marched in" after their children had been assigned "a totally inadequate teacher." "We just had a meeting and we said no, she won't do. She was just totally inexperienced. . . . She was gone within six weeks, and they hired someone else." In both instances, parents intervened actively in the life of the school. But while the latter intervention was focused on the immediate needs of the children of those involved (the human-resource frame), in the former instance it was the school as a whole that stood to benefit from an intervention that was driven by a less self-interested set of values and ideals (a concern of the structural frame).

Understandably, it has been difficult for parents and faculty to sustain this kind of idealism, but as suggested earlier, it is likely that a shift from "founding families" to newcomers has been exaggerated. There still are quite a few parents among the most recent cohorts of families who are no less devoted to the school's general well-being than were the parents who preceded them (although perhaps in less abstract fashion). In recent years, newer parents have been a visible presence as volunteers in the classroom and at lunchtime, in organizing special events, in the parents' association, and even on the board—investing their time in ways that often have little immediate relevance to their own children.

Nevertheless, on those occasions when the school does struggle to recruit volunteers who are willing to give their time on behalf of other people's children, this struggle does seem to be tied to the dynamic of school choice. Families who purposefully chose not to send their children to public school because of skepticism that their goals or needs will be satisfied appear to be just as calculating or individualistic about satisfying their needs once their child is enrolled in a private school.

This, at least, seems to be the impulse behind the following admission from one mother: "With my own kids I went and did art workshops. I was asked to come and do it this year, and I wasn't really motivated since I didn't have enough time. I was sort of willing to make time when my kids were in the class, and less willing to make the time when my kids were not in the classroom they wanted me to work with."

This statement seems to epitomize the challenge in the structural frame of parents' being willing to give their time when they can expect some benefits for their own children but displaying reluctance when their involvement is aimed at the school as an institution. Yet on further examination this statement may not represent a triumph of individualism over altruism. Deborah Conway, the parent who made this admission, had been deeply involved in many aspects of school life since her child began attending DJDS. While it is likely that some of her early idealism had faded, a more significant element in her waning volunteerism is the fact that, as someone who works full-time in her own studio, she has limited time to devote to the school and must volunteer strategically. Under these circumstances she chooses to contribute her time to those activities in which she has direct contact with her own child because she doesn't have much time with her at home.

Another working mother (Anne Wagner, who has a full-time job at a major hospital) gave even more explicit expression to this calculation:

> What I like to do is things that don't take a huge amount of my time. I don't feel that I have very much time. I want to give the time I have to the little people in my life because I work a lot. . . . It's a struggle to find a balance when you're working full-time and you've got two kids. You try to have a life. So that's the struggle. I agreed to serve as a buddy to a new family since it seemed like a relatively easy thing to do and a good thing to do. So when they called, I said sure, fine, I'll do it. But when I was asked if I would like to do challah duty next year, I said no thank you. It seemed like it was too much time for me, so I said, maybe in a couple of years.

The factors that shape parent involvement in the structural frame are complex. Parents, it seems, volunteer strategically on behalf of the school as an institution. They are far from disinterested in the school's general well-being, but they contribute to its welfare while taking account of their own particular resources and needs. At the same time, although they may evince a highly individualistic or consumeristic streak when selecting the school, even those parents who most aggressively "shopped around" before making a choice still seem ready to contribute to the school's general well-being, sometimes before their children even start school. Contrary to appearances, they are not just narrowly concerned with satisfying their own needs.

The challenge for the school is to balance these many commitments and constraints. It is a challenge that the DJDS parents' association has wisely noted. As we came to the end of our time in the school—during the school's seventh year of existence—the PTA resolved to increase parent involvement by creating opportunities for parents to contribute to the school while spending time with their children. They planned to provide more opportunities for parents to organize recess and lunchtime activities, to organize a school play with parent and child participants, to establish a parent association lounge in the school, and to actively encourage parents to participate in *rosh chodesh* [monthly prayer] services with their children.

At the time of writing, the outcome of these initiatives was not yet known, but the initiatives themselves indicate an appreciation of an intersection between the human resources frame and the structural frame that is easily overlooked and that can be a source of great vitality for a school.

The Political Frame: Parents as Governors, Attempting to Shape Policy in Their Children's School

Bolman and Deal characterize the political frame as that wherein "members of an organization, enduringly different from one another in their values, beliefs and interests . . . compete in a state of inevitable conflict . . . for the power to decide who gets what . . . in a situation of scarce resources" (2003, 186). This summation reflects very well much of the interaction between parents and teachers at DJDS, if not in most private schools. It explains also why this relationship is often so turbulent and uncomfortable. As was discussed earlier, although teachers and parents at DJDS share numerous interests, they differ—at least according to many parents—in terms of certain values and beliefs, and, as will be seen later, the school's development and governance places them in a state of conflict with each other.

Like other private schools, DJDS is governed by a board with a large parent presence rather than by a group of outside trustees from the community. In formal terms, parents are invested with a power to make and shape policy that in public settings would be the responsibility of municipal-level appointees. This brings parents into the school often and not infrequently into situations of conflict with teachers and administration. At DJDS, the sense of parent power is deepened further by virtue of the school's origins as an institution created in the front rooms of their homes by parents who, as one of the founders put it, "then had to find an administration that thought like they did." These origins are enduringly symbolized by the presence of the school's "founder"—a parent herself—as a lifetime member of the governing board. Her appointment was made out of respect for her dedication in getting the school started but also, one suspects, so she might serve as a custodian of the school's original vision. This sense of parent influence sees further expression in a view voiced by a substantial minority of parent interviewees that "what makes the school unique is, for the most part, its parent body." As Deborah Conway put it: "The parent body right now drives that desire to be more expansive, more worldly, more diverse, because that's the composition of the parent body. I think that's the most unique thing the school has that other Jewish day schools don't have, and that has attracted a sector of the community who want this but couldn't find it elsewhere."

Significantly, when teachers were asked what in their view made the school special, quite a few suggested that it was the quality and collegiality of the faculty. The parents, some teachers suggested, were much like other private school parents. This different perspective speaks directly to a source of tension in the school but also to a vital source of parental involvement: a difference in opinion between parents and teachers over who makes the school what it is.

For a few parents, one of the factors that has made involvement in the school so appealing is the ease of access to structures that, in formal terms, allow them great power. As one father, Donald Reinhart, put it, this is a fluid environment that has been and can still be molded by parents. Six years on, "the curriculum is still in development," and some school policies are not set in stone. Involvement, from his perspective, can make a difference. For other parents, however, it is their disappointment at not having more influence over matters of policy in an institution encouraging their involvement that led them to withdraw their child from the school after only one year. "The school is marketed as really encouraging parents to be involved in the educational process but they don't. Parents are encouraged to get involved in terms of labor, like volunteering on school trips and organizing events, but not in terms of pedagogy; we're not there" (Samuel Aziz).

Although the outcomes in these two cases may be profoundly different, it is striking that the protagonists were drawn to the school by a similar expectation of having influence over policy matters. Evidently, this is a mixed blessing.

This expectation constitutes one of the many challenges faced by Erica Caplin, the school principal, as she navigates the potentially treacherous, potentially fertile terrain within the political frame. As one parent elaborated, Caplin must "figure out how to engage a group of intelligent and creative people who have a lot of good ideas, without them thinking they can come in and run the school." This is not easy when the parents, committed to their children "directing their own learning in partnership with educators," are also inclined to desire a very high level of partnership for themselves. Further complicating matters is the fact that Caplin's profile makes her suspect in the eyes of those parents who are particularly jealous of the school's downtown identity: she is an Orthodox Jew from outside of the downtown area, in her first senior position, where she is younger than many in the parent body.

According to Caplin, she spends more time talking and listening to parents than on any other single activity. She must attend to those parents who, as Estelle Lombard put it, are "very interested in the arts, very interested in creativity or creative aspects of the school, but feel that these things are falling by the way- side." At the same time, she must respond to those who "are far more interested in academics and curriculum, in making sure that their kids get their math and spelling," what in the context of school discourse has become known as "academic excellence." Some parents come to challenge her over scheduling and work- load decisions—for example, a decision to place some homeroom teachers on part-time rather than full-time contracts, a move made for financial reasons but contested by parents for its poten- tial educational consequences. For a number of months she had to contend with a heated dispute between teachers and parents over the school calendar. The problem for teachers, as one of them explained, was that "you have a parent body who have chosen to go to day school but want a public school calendar." For certain parents, as one mother explained, the problem was that their chil- dren "are at school for a full month less than those in public schools and are expected to cover a double curriculum. . . . They're not doing a double curriculum and they're not doing academic excellence. . . . It's not possible in that time."

These issues and many others have the capacity to generate and absorb hours of parent involvement, on permanent or ad-hoc committees of the school board, in the preparation and organiza- tion of surveys to test parent opinion on these matters, and, less formally but more widely, in hours of telephone conversations and e-mail communications. This intensive activity can have var- ious consequences—some positive, some more problematic. Pos- itively, it solidifies parents' own identities in relation to the school, as they find themselves bombarded (particularly if they're board members) by "the emails, and the be on my side; no, be on my side." Parents soon become identified by the positions they take on issues that may, in fact, have little consequence for their children's learning but may have more significance for where and with whom their loyalties are seen to lie.

Less dramatically, political activity simply gives parents some- thing "to bitch about" when they meet with other parents outside school. For parents who differ from one another in so many ways and can struggle to find common points of connection, these effects are not insignificant. Within the political frame, parents are social-ized in the use of a shared discourse around a common set of con-cerns. "I think I'm the least cliquey person. But certainly I find myself influenced by what people say. I don't know Sandra Meyers [the newly appointed vice principal], but I find myself saying, 'Oh, Sandra Myers, she's amazing!' So far my dealings with her have been quite superficial. She seems professional—that's all I know. But I'm not kidding, I do say, 'Oh Sandra, she's fabulous!' You hear all of these people saying it, maybe because they heard somebody else saying it" (Barb Spencer).

Least positively, this intense political activity—while inspir-ing parents to volunteer more of their time—can also result in parent fatigue and disenchantment. Ultimately, what actually happens in the school is shaped by teachers and faculty by virtue of their daily presence in the building. Few parents have the time or energy to maintain their scrutiny or investment in any issue, no matter how important. (This is a well-known factor in the gen-eral resistance of schools to change [Sarason 1996; Tye 2000].) When parents spend hours of their time on an issue and then find that a different strategy or approach was taken by faculty, their frustration can easily turn to a generalized disaffection with both administration and faculty, and this in turn weakens their invest-ment in the school. As we discuss later, this dynamic runs directly counter to the relationship between parents and teachers created within the other frames of parent involvement.

The Symbolic Frame: Parents as Members of a (Self-) Chosen Community

The three frames described earlier account for a large part of what brings parents into the school or what causes them to invest many hours in their children's education. Yet there are aspects of par-ents' relationships with the school that these frames do not cap-ture. The existence of this extra dimension within parent-school relationships is somewhat counterintuitive given the conven-tional view of schools as institutions that (only) serve children, but it comes clearly into view within what Bolman and Deal (2003) identify as one last frame for analyzing organizational life, what they call the symbolic frame. The symbolic frame is that realm within which organizations attempt to build a culture that gives purpose and meaning through the use of ritual, ceremony, and story (269). Broad in scope, the symbolic frame has implications for parents that may be no less significant than those it has for children. For Jewish parents who have entered the school with an ambivalent relationship to Jewish culture, these implications may have profound sociological implications.

Generally, in schools, the culture-building work of the symbolic frame is most visible when parents come into schools for special occasions convened for the family members of students. These events are a commonplace part of the Jewish day-school landscape across North America. They include occasions to mark landmark events such as the presentation of a first siddur to students or the first time students are called to the Torah. They celebrate special moments from the weekly or annual calendar, with parents participating, for example, in a special havdalah event or a Pesach seder. Less commonly, these events also include ceremonial conclusions to a program of study such as a book of Chumash or a unit of history. As hackneyed as they often seem, these occasions can serve as powerful vehicles for articulating core school values and for helping people bond with them; they can help families develop a shared institutional narrative with other members of the school community, and they can gently socialize parents into the rhythms of the Jewish year.

These kinds of public events are held frequently at DJDS. The family Chanukah program, the school book fair, the Parent Association Oneg Shabbat, and a series of events before Passover constitute some of the most beloved occasions in the school year. As we discuss in the next chapter, they are inspiring moments for both parents and children when "the magic at DJDS" is felt most strongly.

Impressively, and in contrast to many other (Jewish) schools, faculty at DJDS are generally alert to the possibility that these events (as expressions of the symbolic frame) may possess meaning for parents' own lives beyond their role as vehicles for children's education (an aspect of the human resource frame) or as devices for displaying what has been achieved at school (a dimension of the structural frame). This alertness derives from an awareness among teachers of two gaps: one between most parents' own experience of schooling and that of their children, and a second between the Jewish content of school life and the Jewish content of children's lives outside school. These gaps are evidenced most publicly at school open houses when prospective parents ask, for example, whether they can send their child to the school if they themselves don't believe in God or if they have trouble expressing support for the State of Israel. Teachers, it seems, recognize that what children encounter in school and take home has the potential to disturb the equilibrium of parents' lives. Thus they must be ready, even as early as senior kindergarten, to respond to parents' questions about material they cover or ideas they introduce not only because parents seek to facilitate their children's learning of these things but also because parents want to learn about them themselves.

Joanna Fried, the kindergarten teacher, describes in detail how she has responded to parent inquiries and questions, thereby making parents active participants in the curriculum in their own homes.

> When we do our unit on houses and homes we talk a little bit about our Jewish homes and what makes your home a Jewish home. I remember having a parent who said, well, what happens if you have nothing Jewish in your home. (This was a parent who was at an open house who actually sent her child here in the end.) I said everybody has something in their home that shows that they're Jewish. Do you have a *kippah* hidden somewhere in your home or something in your pantry that shows that it's a kosher item? Whether or not you bought it because it was kosher, there is a kosher item somewhere in your house and you can connect it to Judaism in that way.
>
> So we created a Shabbat box with a Kiddush cup and candlestick and a little stuffed animal with the *kippah* and a song sheet and the *brachot* and a tzedakah box and they get to do challot and each child gets a turn to take the Shabbat box home and celebrate Shabbat in their house whichever way they want to.

Experiences like these in kindergarten that are grounded in a nonjudgmental stance toward the Jewish lives of families encourage parents to see the school as a place where they too can belong and where they can learn about Judaism without being intimidated or judged. These are not outcomes typically expected from parents' relationships with their children's schools, but such outcomes reflect two previously unconsidered dimensions of significance in the relationships between Jewish parents and their children's schools that come into view within the symbolic frame. These dimensions—consequences of the culture-building content of the symbolic frame—raise important questions about the role of day schools in contemporary Jewish life. We will explore these two dimensions more fully in the following two chapters because they take us to the heart of our inquiry at DJDS, but we first introduce them here against the backdrop of the symbolic frame.

The first dimension, what we call "the school as shul," reflects the extent to which, for many DJDS parents, the school—as a creator of Jewish culture—serves needs satisfied historically (for North American Jews) by synagogues as houses of worship, meeting, and study.

In some instances the school (literally) acts as a substitute for the synagogue by providing a surrogate community. As Joanna Fine explained: "I couldn't see myself ever going to regular Saturday morning services, and quite frankly I'm not that keen on sitting through services and I think my children would hate it. But the nice thing about the DJDS is you have a community for celebrating those things. And when you're not affiliated with a synagogue you'd have to otherwise make a special effort."

In other instances, parents depend on the school to provide some of the religious "services" one would ordinarily expect from a synagogue. In the oldest grades, for example, parents turn to the homeroom teacher for her advice about how to celebrate their child's upcoming bar/bat mitzvah, an event that for many Jews in North America can be the only point of connection between families and synagogue life (Schoenfeld 1990). Polly Tolman, the fifth-grade teacher, as it happens, is an accomplished Torah chanter and is capable of teaching children their Torah portion much as a rabbi might.

More subtly, for those members of the parent body who tend to be on the edges of the mainstream Jewish community—converts to Judaism, gay couples, interfaith families—involvement in the school provides the possibility of self-affirmation, of participating as a valued member of the community, when this is rarely possible in other Jewish institutions or even within their own extended families. This sense of inclusion is most powerfully conveyed by the participation of non-Jewish parents on the school's governing board and as chairs on some of the board's most influential sub-committees. It is also communicated less formally in the kinds of conversations conducted in classrooms and corridors where parents talk of "not having been excluded . . . as a result of not being Jewish" or because of being recently converted. These are the kinds of experiences that other North American Jews seek within their synagogues and temples but that many DJDS families do not find in such settings because of their often ambivalent relationships to organized religion or because of their nontraditional family structures. The school in these respects satisfies many of the spiritual, social, and intellectual needs of parents in ways that are either analogous or directly equivalent to those provided by the synagogue. These are significant consequences that we explore more fully in the next chapter.

A second dimension of the symbolic frame that calls for further examination is what we call "the school at home." In this case, meanings and values constructed at school are experienced by parents not within the school's physical space but within parents' own homes, through the mediation of their own children.

We sense from our interviews with parents, children, and teachers at DJDS that children, and their school experiences, create portals to Jewish life for parents, much as, parents say, their own grandparents did for them when they were children. If, in their childhood, their grandparents, who were frequently immigrants, provided them with the occasions and content of Jewish life, now it is their own children who recite blessings for them, instruct them in what to say at a seder, and invite them to mark Shabbat. This is what we mean by the notion of the school at home.

Parents give expression to this phenomenon by talking frequently about "living Judaism through their children." They indicate thereby that they experience Judaism through the initiative and mediation of their children. This does not mean, however, that they necessarily embrace or adopt whatever their children bring into their homes. As we describe in chapter 5, children introduce new practices and rituals into their family homes on Friday nights and Jewish holidays, or they simply express themselves in Hebrew at unexpected moments, and parents must choose to adopt, adapt, or reject these interruptions. In certain respects, parents must decide how they respond to these interruptions no less purposefully than they must choose how to involve themselves inside the school. Their response at home is as much a mode of involvement as is volunteering at school.

Although in conventional sociological terms the family is regarded as the most powerful mediating influence on the quality of children's school experience, children also bring ideas from school into their homes that can in turn have an impact on the life of the family. We find that children internalize messages in the classroom that can inform how parents conceive of their relationships to the school community and to the Jewish community beyond the school. In these cases, the school's influence starts in the classroom, in relationships and conversations between teachers and students, where teachers communicate to students that they are respected and taken seriously whatever Jewish practices they observe at home. These ideas find a receptive audience when carried home. They provide parents with a license to explore and develop their own understandings of what it means to be a Jewish family or of what constitutes authentic Jewish practice. In turn, children bring into the classroom from their homes diverse expressions of Jewish life and family life that shape teachers' understandings and practices as well as the kinds of classroom communities they nurture. At home, the Jewish culture created by the school is reproduced, reconstructed, and in time reflected back to the classroom.

In their various settings, at home and at school, the involvements of the symbolic frame possess a sociocultural significance that goes beyond parents' immediate concern with their own children and their children's teachers. If the human resource frame is focused on the needs of children, and if the institutional and political frames are focused on those of the school as an organization, the symbolic frame's focus on the development of culture and shared meaning has implications for the Jewish community as a whole.

The symbolic frame, by making space for the development of shared culture, nurtures a sense of belonging that exists in sharp contrast to the feelings of tension and conflict fostered by the political frame. Unlike in the political frame, where parents and teachers constitute rival sources of power competing for control of the school, the symbolic frame provides a space for the interaction of different cultures and for the development of shared language and commitments. It is our sense that this process of cultural construction occurs both within the school (in ways that resemble the prominent and public features of synagogue life) and more privately in family homes (where parents and children engage in what one might call the subatomic work of cultural construction). In the following chapters we explore what these processes mean for the lives of the Jewish adults whose children attend the school, and then in our final chapters we investigate more broadly what might be the consequences and implications of these phenomena for contemporary Jewish society.

The School as Shul

JEWISH DAY SCHOOLS
AS PLACES OF WORSHIP,
STUDY, AND ASSEMBLY,
FOR PARENTS

As we discussed in the last chapter, the symbolic frame refers to that social realm within which culture is built. It is where, through ritual, ceremony, and story, groups, organizations, and societies find shared purpose and meaning.

For Jews, the two institutions that, more than any others, have performed these culture-building roles are the family and the synagogue. The family, according to Goodkind (1994), has "throughout Jewish history . . . been the center from which all else emanates: Jewish education, involvement with the community, religious celebrations and observance, and Jewish identity and continuity" (vii). The synagogue, in Schorsch's graphic image, "is the bedrock institution of the total Jewish community. . . . While its ritual is a bridge to the divine, it is also a force for cohesion and the language of social values" (cited by Wertheimer 2005).

In the next chapter we explore the intersection between families and the school, examining how within their own homes DJDS families adopt, adapt, and reject what their children learn at school. In this chapter we take up a set of sociological lenses more typically employed to study "synagogue life" to examine to what extent there are parallels to the synagogue's functions within the symbolic frame of school life, that is, within the ways parents find meaning and purpose inside their children's school.

Historically, the synagogue has been identified as performing three primary sociological functions: (1) as a site for social fellowship, indicated by the etymological root of the Greek word *synagogue*, meaning "place of assembly" (Kaufman 1999); (2) as an educational institution, symbolized by the vernacular Yiddish term *shul*, literally meaning "school" (Heilman 1976); and (3) as a place of religious worship, the synagogue's original function in the ancient world, according to Levine (1987). In modern times, with the emergence of what Kaplan called the "synagogue center," these elements have merged, with synagogues taking on the role of multifunctional institutions, trying to attract as much of the Jewish marketplace as possible (Sklare [1955] 1972). Nevertheless, despite this recent fusion of roles, the long-term vitality of these institutions still seems to depend on how well they can serve the discrete religious, educational, and social needs of their members.

In this chapter we take up the themes revealed by earlier chapters to develop a thesis about the ways in which DJDS exhibits the three functions traditionally performed by the synagogue as *bet kenesset* (house of meeting), *bet midrash* (house of study), and *bet tephilah* (house of prayer). In general sociological terms this line of inquiry can be situated within literature that examines how Jews construct and negotiate their identities in alternative ways, that is to say, outside the traditional locale of the synagogue. Davidman (2003), for example, engaged this theme of identity "beyond the synagogue walls" in her examination of American Jews who are unaffiliated with a synagogue yet take their Jewish identities seriously and exert significant effort in creating and maintaining their Jewishness. Prell (1989) also looked beyond the traditional synagogue in her ethnographic study of a Los Angeles *havurah*, an alternative, informal, egalitarian prayer group that placed special focus on individual experience and meaning. Grant (2001) studied how adult Jewish identities come to be reworked within the context of adult educational trips to Israel. Schwartz (1988), meanwhile, stayed closer to home to explore how the family seder night serves as a site for the construction and negotiation of complex Jewish identities.

Our chapter, along with these earlier studies, implicitly asks the question of whether institutions other than the traditional synagogue can successfully connect with adults inclined to look for and find Jewish meaning as an extension of the personal, intimate sphere. This question, we suggest, has become especially pertinent given the fact that synagogue membership has significantly decreased in the United States from the postwar period (when 60 percent of Jews claimed membership) to a level today of 46 percent (Wertheimer 2005).

In empirical terms, instead of returning to the interview data from which we previously drew, we present a series of vignettes derived from field-site observations at the school. Through these ethnographic portraits of the school we attempt to make explicit how the behaviors and outcomes identified in previous chapters can be directly attributed to the school serving for parents as a house of social fellowship, education, and spiritual inspiration. While these elements can be neatly divided into these three categories, in reality, and as will be seen, these features often fuse together in both synagogues and schools.

Bet Kenesset: The School as a Site for Social Fellowship

As a religiously pluralist day school, DJDS is more inclusive than other schools in the Toronto area, especially in relation to those who fall outside either familiar denominational and religious categories or traditional family structures. As alluded to in chapter 1, more than one-third of the children in the school have parents who are intermarried, converts to Judaism, in same-sex relationships, in a common-law relationship, or single. For many of these parents the school serves as a type of Jewish haven, one of the only Jewish institutions where they feel completely at liberty to be themselves. One parent, writing to a school committee, explained that her family "had suffered immeasurably when they left [their egalitarian] synagogue after finding [that their lesbian union] didn't qualify as a 'family.'" In contrast, she emphasized, DJDS had made no such judgments about her life. This attitude of pluralism, which permeates throughout the school, helps to foster an environment of belonging or social fellowship.

A number of other comments confirm that factors deriving from parents' own particular identities play a role in how comfortable they feel within their children's school environment. As we saw in chapter 2 when discussing parents' journeys to the school, one couple explained how important it was that this was a school where other parents also had children late in life. Another couple indicated that they were drawn to being at a school with families who shared their values (making charitable donations rather than buying gifts for friends' birthdays) and who dressed like them (enabling them to attend school meetings in cycle gear). As one interviewee memorably put it, this was a place where they found other "downtown schlumpy Jews" like themselves. For one parent, the Jewish partner in an interfaith marriage, it was important to give her child and herself a Jewish connection. As we noted previously, the school offers parents and their children what Merz and Furman (1997) call communities of kinship, neighborhood, and mind. The school "fits" with many significant aspects of who they are.

Vignette A: The Board as Community

Schnoor was fortunate to have the opportunity to spend two full years as an observer of all the monthly meetings of the school's eighteen-member board of directors. Attendance at these meetings allowed him as a researcher to maintain a healthy relationship with the school's important gatekeepers and also to keep the board up-to-date with the long-term research project. Schnoor's many hours of observing the interactions of board meetings revealed a previously unconsidered source of social fellowship: the power of the school board to create social cohesiveness among parents.

A sense of this power can be gained by reading two of his field notes:

Field Notes, School Board Meeting, January 26, 2006

As I have attended several board meetings now over the course of many months it has occurred to me that the monthly meetings of the school's board of directors, along with the initiatives and activities of the board, serve as an important vehicle for

Jewish bonding. For Jews, many of whom do not belong to a synagogue, being involved on their children's school board serves as a key source of Jewish engagement. It provides a tremendous sense of friendship and camaraderie. I must admit that I even feel a warm sense of being part of an accepting community, and I am only a researcher observing the meetings. This work constitutes a monthly visit to the Jewish Community Centre to do important Jewish things with Jewish friends and colleagues (a kind of monthly *rosh chodesh* service). Even more so than attending regular prayers services, however, the actions performed and decisions that these people make have important consequences for a Jewish institution. The sense of belonging to a team that's working toward a common Jewish cause is a very powerful feeling. The self-satisfaction of helping a Jewish institution thrive, an institution where your children are educated and socialized, cannot be overstated. By serving on the board, the school seems to be less about the children. It feels more like an institution of and for the parents [and perhaps of the Jewish community beyond].

Field Notes, School Board Meeting, February 16, 2006

This month I received added confirmation about the ability of the DJDS board to provide parents with a strong sense of Jewish connection and solidarity. This became particularly evident when at tonight's meeting, a long-standing board member announced that he would be stepping down and that this would be his last meeting. Sammy, a professional accountant, served as treasurer for three years and demonstrated tremendous commitment and leadership on the board on many issues. I witnessed this myself. He is very well spoken and well respected. The pleas for him to stay on the board and the effusive praise for him demonstrated the tight-knit bonds that form among board members. The cause of running the school brings these people together in a sense of collective duty and responsibility. It is different than running a commercial corporation; running a Jewish school seems to have much more cultural, emotional, and personal value to these people. I could tell that losing Sammy's presence on the board was like losing a member of one's family. The board acts as a mini Jewish community for these parents. It is like an extension of their Jewish family.

The board's annual general meeting in April 2006 emphasized the same themes. Each member of the board who was resigning, including Sammy, was asked to come to the front of the room where he or she was effusively thanked and eloquently praised by the board copresident and given a plaque in recognition of his or her services. Rousing applause followed each presentation, some board members even rising in their seats while applauding. In turn each retiring board member gave a speech about how much this experience had meant to him or her personally. Clearly, the school had made a strong impact on their own adult identities as Jews, as evidenced by the speakers reflecting on how the school provided them with a "community" or "a new way of thinking about religion." One board member reiterated these thoughts by saying how he "fell in love with the culture of the school." The reflections and sentiments often had nothing to do with the children in the school, at least not directly. It seemed as if the parents were celebrating their own individual and collective achievements.

Vignette B: Parents Plead for More School

Another strong demonstration of the importance of the school in the lives of parents came in early 2006 when a crucial decision needed to be made as to whether or not the school was going to expand to a middle school (which includes the seventh and eighth grades) in the following school year. This had been a long-standing issue in the young life of the school. High school does not begin until ninth grade, and many parents always had the desire to offer a senior-kindergarten-through-eighth-grade program. Costs and other logistical challenges had until this point prevented the school from achieving this goal. But by June 2005 the school had reached an important milestone: the first group of children graduated from the sixth grade, and parents were forced into a difficult decision as to where to place them for the two years before high school. During the middle of the 2005–6 school year a groundswell of support developed among the parents of the sixth-grade students to help establish a middle school program at DJDS. These parents formed a team with some of the parents of recent DJDS graduates whose children were already in seventh-grade programs elsewhere in the city and who were interested in bringing their children back to the school they loved.

This energetic parent campaign culminated in a January 2006 school board meeting where twelve non-board-member parents were invited to attend and share their views about the potential middle school. The board insisted that by the end of the meeting a final decision would have to be made as to whether the middle school could or could not become a reality the following school year. Schnoor attended this meeting for what was in his opinion one of the most dramatic field visits he experienced in his more than three years observing the school. In turn, each parent gave a stirring account of why they loved the school and why they wanted their children to remain or return. Each speech was more inspiring than the next. In glowing terms the parents described the school as the only place that promotes their downtown Jewish values and, after experiencing open houses and programs at other "alternative" schools, the only place in the city where *they* felt truly comfortable. Parents effusively praised Sandra Meyers, the newly appointed school principal, explaining how they were inspired by her educational vision for the middle school. It was an impressive display of passion for their children's school. Clearly, these parents had developed a deep personal connection to the school community. Referring to the emotional sixth-grade graduation ceremony of the previous summer, one seventh-grade parent admitted, "Leaving last year was the hardest thing *I* ever did!" Another parent looked around at the other parents in the room and made the heart-felt declaration that "these are all my friends that *I* made in senior kindergarten!" Rounds of applause followed from the board members.

While there was widespread enthusiasm for the project from both the parent presenters and members of the board, serious financial challenges stood in the way of making the middle school a reality. This pressing issue consumed much of the discussion. In the end a deal was struck: the parents agreed to pay $1,000 more than the standard school tuition of $12,350 for 2006–7. Furthermore, they made a pledge that they would independently raise an additional $90,000. One parent dramatically pledged that she would sell the expensive Persian rug from her own living room floor. Another, a professional photographer, promised to sell his valuable photo exhibit of downtown synagogues.

After one of the longest board meetings in school history (concluding at 11:30 PM), the board made the momentous decision to endorse the middle school initiative. These Jewish adults, many of whom by their own admission had never before been members of any Jewish organization as either children or adults, had successfully come together to enable their children to stay in a Jewish day school for another two years. Their joint project, as lobbyists and activists, speaks volumes about the role the school plays in their own social lives.

Bet Midrash: The School as a Site for Adult Learning

There is a widespread assumption that adults only learn in schools when instruction is programmed in family or adult-education events. At DJDS, we found that parents rarely attended formally programmed adult education events but instead engaged in learning in numerous unpredictable and informal ways. In the course of conducting business at a variety of school committees, parents worked hard to extend their understanding of a range of Jewish and educational issues so that they could make informed decisions about, for example, how to market the school or who to invite as classroom visitors. We discovered also that aspects of the school's curriculum often provoked parents to come in to talk with the school's educators about theological and philosophical issues. The curriculum not only enabled them to learn how to perform unfamiliar Jewish practices (such as welcoming the Sabbath in their homes or building a *Sukkah*) but also provoked them to reconsider deeply rooted and previously unchallenged assumptions about Judaism and life.

Vignette C: Reassessing Bible Stories

Before considering some of the larger implications of these consequences, it is possible to gain a more nuanced sense of what parents "learned" from the school in the following vignette extracted from an interview with the school's founding principal, Jessica Steinberg. Steinberg served as principal at DJDS for the school's first three years, while continuing to act as principal of a local part-time Hebrew school that she had founded more than twenty years previously. She was deeply committed to the success of DJDS and the development of the downtown Jewish community, but her involvement was something of an emergency measure to help get the school started.

More than a year after stepping down as principal, Steinberg provided a measured consideration of the school's special characteristics. Toward the end of the pilot study Pomson requested her perspective on many features of the school's development and also on some of the provisional conclusions about what we had observed (Pomson 2004).

In the following excerpt from their conversation, Steinberg offers her view of the school's influence on parents' lives.

> JS: I think there were parents who came into the school having some negative feelings about Judaism. They felt that it was superstitious, that it was childish, that it lacked sophistication in terms of theology and philosophy, and I think that that changed. I think in certain circumstances that changed. The whole concept of metaphor—parents didn't understand the concept of God and metaphor. So I think that it changed some people who started out thinking that they were secular Jews.
>
> AP: What was it about the school that changed them? Was it the kinds of experiences they saw their kids having or was it . . . ?
>
> JS: It was their own involvement.
>
> AP: The conversations they had as adults?
>
> JS: It was their own involvement. And sometimes it was an experience that their child had that would start the involvement. Concerned that . . . about a Bible story the child had brought home, and having all these sorts of inner conflicts come out about what their child is learning.
>
> AP: People would bring those concerns to you?
>
> JS: Yes. And then . . .
>
> AP: I just wonder where they would encounter those theological issues.

JS: Yes, I talked to parents about theology and would also encourage them to join the Religious Policy and Planning Committee, where we talked in depth about it.

AP: Did you find yourself having many conversations with parents?

JS: Yes. And I loved it.

AP: That's interesting. That's not something that I . . .

JS: They came angry. They came angry. I think from their childhood experiences and just feeling that grown-ups don't—this is not something for grown-ups—and they didn't want their children to get the "Bubbe meises" that they [heard as children].

Steinberg's comments confirm something that is well known: parents bring baggage to their children's schools, a set of emotion-laden assumptions about Judaism and education derived from their own childhoods, and often unchallenged since then. These preconceptions are analogous to the "institutional knowledge" teacher candidates bring to teacher education programs from their own experiences of schooling (Britzman 1991; Lortie 1975). They constitute a set of deeply embedded and often conservative ideas about teaching, learning, and curriculum that derive from many hours spent in classrooms as students. What is less well known but is suggested by Steinberg's remarks is that these long-held ideas can be challenged by encounters between parents and their children's schools even when their children are quite young. In this instance, the parents who came to the principal with theological questions and reassessed their views of themselves as secular Jews were responding to aspects of the curriculum encountered by children who were not more than eight years old at the time. We observe that in a certain sense they turned to the school principal much as synagogue members would turn to their rabbi for education and counseling on religious or spiritual matters.

How and why parents were inspired to turn to the principal in this way is not clarified by the conversation. Pomson had imagined that there was some vicarious influence at work in which parents reassessed their own ideas in light of their children's experiences. Tantalizingly, Steinberg points to another transformational dynamic, something she calls the parents' "own involvement." Although this was a notion Pomson didn't attend to when Steinberg first mentioned it, we saw in the previous chapter that the investment of parents' selves in their children's education is a key concept in making sense of the relationships between parents and their children's schools.

Active parent involvement in the school can help provide a significant educational dimension to parents' school experience, or, to be more precise, to their experience of their children's school. And as will be demonstrated in the following vignette, this educational payoff is often fused with the previously described benefit of finding community through social fellowship.

Vignette D: Drama at the Religious and Educational Policy Committee

One of the most fertile venues for adult involvement in the school is the board's Religious and Educational Policy Committee (REPC). This committee is made up of a diverse group that includes parents, members of the downtown Jewish community, grandparents, and the school's two senior administrators. At the start of our research, the committee had just been reconstituted under the leadership of two new chairs whose profiles convey something of the nontraditional demographics of the school: one is the non-Jewish parent in an interfaith family; the other—a person with extensive experience in a variety of Jewish educational settings—is a partner and parent in a same-sex relationship.

At the first of the year's meetings, the chairs worked carefully to develop inclusive and effective procedures for the committee's operation. In late November they devoted the year's first substantive meeting to a discussion of the school's policy on religious pluralism. This did not produce any major action items but rather led to a commitment to "communicate" existing policies to parents through workshops and to "explain how teachers practice pluralism."

Within a week of this meeting, however, the chairs convened what they described as an "emergency" meeting to respond to questions raised by a distraught parent about the school's "commitment to diversity," the very matter considered by the committee at its previous meeting. These questions were provoked by the scheduling of a pre-Chanukah event in the school to be led by a local rabbi (Rabbi Sternfeld) whose opinions (at least as far as could be determined from his institutional affiliations) were viewed as "blatantly intolerant of and hostile to" minority groups within the school. Writing as a gay member of the school community, this parent asked others "to entertain the anguish that many feel in being asked to honor the 'rights' of others who actively seek to diminish or erase our own rights." This parent was the previously mentioned individual who "had suffered immeasurably" at her synagogue when her same-sex relationship did not qualify as a "family."

In the days before the "emergency" meeting, communicating largely by e-mail, members of the committee articulated their responses to the issues provoked by this parent's appeal to withdraw Rabbi Sternfeld's invitation. Our account of this episode draws on e-mail transcripts circulated between committee members before the meeting and field notes taken during and after it.

This episode has all of the qualities of a "social drama" as originally conceived by Turner (1974) and applied by Reimer (1997) to the study of culture in Jewish schools. The episode began with a "breach"—"the public non-fulfillment of some crucial norm regulating the intercourse of . . . parties" (Turner 1974, 38)—when the parent challenged the school's practices and what she called its "fluctuating philosophies." This breach quickly became a "crisis," when the chairs called an "emergency" meeting of the REPC. In so doing they did not limit the breach but extended its impact by suggesting that this moment called for the consideration of difficult questions about "how we define and understand Jewish religious pluralism" and "what obligation we have toward protecting the rights, safety and dignity of all our students and families."

Turner suggests that a third phase in social dramas is one of "redressive action." This occurs when "leading or structurally representative members of the disturbed social system" act to limit the spread of the crisis through the use of a variety of mechanisms that "may range from personal advice and informal mediation . . . to the performance of public ritual" (Turner 1974, 39). In this instance the chairperson of the school board as well as some of the REPC members introduced into the discussion a way to recognize the points of difference between Rabbi Sternfeld and most of the school's families, while enabling him, "if he has something valuable to share," to come into the school, provided he "respects every child and parent—our diversity."

This course of action offered a route toward "reintegration," a final phase in the social drama that involved the committee working on collectively acceptable language for a revised policy on religious pluralism. This course of action was also preceded, during the "liminal" phases of the drama, by another subtle but powerful form of redressive action, what Turner identifies as "the performance of public ritual."

In a number of contributions to the e-mail exchange, committee members reminded their colleagues that the discussion— what had originally been called the "emergency"—was itself a reflection of values within the school that called for celebration. As one member put it, "It is a credit to our school that such discussion could be pursued and constructive solutions sought out." For another member, in a beautifully crafted letter, it was precisely the values that had seemed threatened by this crisis (and which she proceeded to rearticulate with great clarity) that provided a guide for how to construct policy in this case.

It is worth quoting at length from this particular committee member's statement because it demonstrates how social dramas can serve as opportunities for reaffirming group loyalties. The letter begins with a reminder of the school's core values and of what the author calls its vision. "I love our school and I am very proud of the community we have built together. We are diverse and yet we stand together, supporting each other as we craft a thoughtful and exciting vision."

As the author goes on to indicate, it was precisely in the consistent performance of these values that a course of action for this difficult situation was suggested.

At DJDS we teach our children respect for diversity. Respect means treating people as worthy or cherished human beings. We do not generalize or label but meet people on their own terms. And we have the same respect for guests we bring into our school. . . . As a school community we recognize that Jewish families and Jewish practice exist on a continuum and, as far as I see it, we don't lightly dismiss someone as "off the continuum." As with most attempts to draw a sharp distinction between the good "us" and the bad "other," the delegitimization of Rabbi Sternfeld, and Orthodoxy in general, ignores the fact that what we share in common is so much more significant than what separates us. . . . Our school is a haven where exclusion and denigration of other Jews is not okay.

Perhaps it is not surprising, given the constructive—one might say "devotional"—tone of the later contributions to the e-mail exchange, that by the time the committee met much of the tension had dissipated, and the drama had moved into a final phase of "reintegration." Although some members of the committee were still pained by what the rabbi's presence implied for their own identities as Jews, there was a general sense within the committee that the discussion had helped members develop or discover their shared values. Indeed, it was agreed that this "traumatic" experience had helped the committee come much closer to developing a stance toward pluralism than had the discussion at the committee's regularly scheduled meeting.

As we have tried to convey, this episode resonates with Turner's characterization of an emergent social drama as a mirror in which the members of a society can view and even discover their shared values and commitments. From a research perspective, this drama also serves as a window on the often submerged values and motivations of the school community.

Evidently the school is not only a vehicle for teaching children but also a site for adult learning. As one member of the committee wrote toward the end of the e-mail discussion, "This has turned into the most incredible learning experience for me. I am not sure I have a strong feeling of what the committee should decide on this issue, but I sure am grateful to have been part of this very informative dialogue." Significantly, for this person, the policy question (the ostensible business of the committee) was secondary to what she learned from the drama about Jewish values and ideas. This was not an unusual reaction. Pomson's field notes from the e-mail exchange and from the committee meeting are filled with references to the richness of the learning, as members swapped reading recommendations and contributed subtle distinctions to one another's ideas. The mood of the discussion may have been emotional, but, in effect, it was not unlike a university seminar on the topics of pluralism, Hasidism, and contemporary Judaism.

The drama thus reveals two powerful aspects to the school's role in the lives of parents. In addition to supplying them with a valuable Jewish educational experience, the school also provides many parents with a sense of community they cannot find in other Jewish institutions. In these respects, the school is distinguished from most other arenas for adult Jewish involvement. For these downtown Jews, many of whom are alienated from denominational Jewish life, DJDS is not only a place where they and their children can learn but also a place where they can belong. It provides a vehicle for realizing a vision of a different kind of Jewish community, a community that sometimes verges on the utopian; or as sociologists of religion classically put it, it is a setting where they experience intimations of the ultimate (James 1902/2002; Otto 1965).

Bet Tephilah: The School as a Site of Religious and Spiritual Inspiration

"Intimations of the ultimate" points to one further significant dimension within parents' investment in the school. This is not so much concerned with what the school *is* but with what parents hope it will *become*. A vein of utopianism runs through the way many parents talk about the school; they frequently speak as though the school is possessed of unlimited potential, sometimes with complete disregard for mundane factors such as staff turnover and budgetary constraints. Perhaps this is typical of how people imagine newly launched schools, where there seem to be few limitations on what they promise. But it may also indicate something more—that at DJDS, an institution that was explicitly founded as an "alternative" day school, many parents have developed a sense of what Turner calls *communitas,* or "a special feeling of connectedness and potentiality that arises when the structures and hierarchies of everyday life are temporarily suspended" (cited by Kirschenblatt-Gimblett n.d., 277).

For Turner, *communitas* is a liminal condition, characteristic of utopian projects; it exists in a "kind of institutional capsule or pocket which contains the germ of future social developments, of societal change" (1982, 45). In his terms it is usually a temporary state that calls for and provides a deep sense of investment and a heightened sense of belonging, much like what we have seen in the behaviors and talk of DJDS parents who have invested themselves in a model of Jewish education and community that differs significantly from the local norm. *Communitas,* Turner argues, occurs at instants of pure potentiality and cultural creativity (1982, 44), like those associated with the early years of a newly created school. It is accompanied by a removal of boundaries between members of the group as they become submerged in a charismatic moment, creating through their investments an alternative way of being (1982, 50–21).

Vignette E: School Ceremonies

When we started our research in the school and began to share findings from the field, colleagues suggested that the intense emotional environment we encountered and the deep parental investment we observed were no doubt products of the school's newness—its liminal condition, as Turner would put it. In time, we were told, the school would evolve from a charismatic state to something more mundane.

We are alert to this critique in presenting the following sets of field notes from a couple of events on the school calendar. These episodes, a graduation ceremony and the annual Chanukah performance, constitute charismatic moments, peak experiences, that provide parents with religious or spiritual inspiration fused with a strong sense of social fellowship with other parents and families. As will be revealed by Schnoor's field notes, the first event invites interpretation as a liminal moment in the evolution of a new school, but the second episode, because it has become a beloved fixed point on the annual calendar, calls for a different explanation. It suggests that less obvious forces may also lie behind the first event's power.

Field Notes, Sixth-Grade Graduation, June 21, 2005

As the first ever graduation ceremony, this was a momentous event for the young school. It was the culmination of seven years of hard work as the small group of children had completed their studies and were moving on to seventh grade at other schools. I knew coming into the Jewish Community Centre party room this pleasant June evening that this would be a festive occasion, but I must admit I was still not fully prepared for the emotionally charged experience that transpired. A representative of the local Jewish Board of Education spoke effusively of the school as a shining light in the downtown Jewish core. The five extroverted and talented graduates performed a tremendous show of skits and heart-felt speeches of thanks to the school and teachers and the approximately sixty-five members of family and friends present. The students' speeches emphasized themes of "nobody is afraid to be themselves" and "we feel at home here like a family." There was a standing ovation for Carrie Lowenstein, the founding parent of the school. It was a true collective celebration of the school. People were laughing and crying. The ceremony finished with fifteen minutes of spontaneous *horas* where the whole audience joined the graduates in festive singing and dancing. I could not help but feel touched and inspired myself.

It is tempting to attribute the emotive power in this event to its lack of precedent, to its marking a significant milestone in the school's development. In new schools, the first and oldest grade is often called the "frontier year." With the first graduation of a sixth-grade class, a frontier had been closed. This event therefore marked a moment of transition from a state of not-yet-fulfilled potential to one of closure that made it particularly poignant. And yet, as we reflect on the intensity and joy we encountered in this and in other less unusual school celebrations, we are inclined to see additional and no less important forces at work, as we suggest after presenting an account of another peak moment from the school calendar.

Field Notes, Annual Chanukah Performance, December 22, 2005

If the Jewish day school can play a similar role as the synagogue in fostering adult Jewish identity, then it strikes me that the annual Chanukah performance must be as significant as *kol nidre* night at the synagogue. This is the one day in the calendar year that practically every parent, grandparent, friend, and supporter of the school come together at the same time to celebrate the school. Durkheim's concept of collective effervescence comes to mind. Through the enthusiasm of the students' presentations, the total group is infused with a collective Jewish spirit greater than the sum of the individual parts. With this type of captive audience and Jewishly charged environment, representatives of the school must choose their words carefully; this is their opportunity to convey to the group what they feel is their most important message. Just as *kol nidre* nights in some congregations are associated with their fund-raising drives to raise money for Israel or other Jewish causes, so at the DJDS Chanukah performances (from 2003 to 2005, I have now witnessed three) the first order of the afternoon is always an inspirational speech about the need to provide financial support to the school. With wealthy potential donors like grandparents and other community friends present, this is the time to make an impact.

As a place where Jewish parents use the school as a key vehicle for adult Jewish identity, I was struck for the second Chanukah in a row by parents choosing to perform at their children's play. If the school is similar to a shul, then a school Chanukah performance bears similarity to a prayer service. Andrea Rappoport, head of the parents' association (and former piano bar and nightclub performer) organized a quartet of women who presented a rapturous and melodious rendition of "Ma'oz Tzur." Their beautiful voices—all in harmony—floated to the rafters of the theater. I shivered as I would when experiencing the music of a shul choir or a talented chazzan.

What is a synagogue service without some words of Jewish wisdom? A particularly articulate second-grade student was chosen to introduce his class's performance. His solemn words around common themes of "the importance of connecting our Jewish lives and spirit to the rich heritage of our Jewish past" and "working together toward *tikkun olam* and peace in the world" couldn't have inspired more emotion had a rabbi spoken them. Though the children's performances were not quite as dynamic and creative as in years past (probably due to the turnover of the school's music teacher), I was still emotionally affected by their show and I do not even have a child there! What Jewish pride for a parent! Their children are both exhibiting their own Jewish identity as absorbed through their experiences at the school and transmitting this Jewishness to their largely Jewishly unaffiliated audience. The show ended with a bang as the crowd rose in rhythmic applause. Their children climbed the stairs to the rear of the theater, excitedly making their way to their classrooms where their parents would join them.

It is worth thinking carefully about what accounts for the force of this event, if only because such force is often missing from similar occasions in other schools where these annual events can seem stale or forced. At DJDS, we find three ingredients that make this event and others like it so meaningful for parents.

Tension: Tension surrounds performances at most schools, where parents wonder whether or not after long hours of rehearsal their children will let them(selves) down. In a school where, as we have seen, so much store has been placed in the desire to do things differently by bringing a downtown quality to the life of a Jewish day school, parents and other audience members share an additional concern: Will this performance properly reflect the special values at the school, or will it look much like similar events on the calendar at other schools? Ironically, the tension produced by such concerns (and the emotional release engendered by their successful resolution) intensifies from one year to the next as performers and audience wonder not only whether they can surpass last year's efforts but also, more subtly, whether with the passage of time from the school's founding the newest generations can remain faithful to the school's founding vision. We expect that future graduation events will have to match and perhaps surpass the memories created by the first one.

Blurred boundaries: The logistical arrangements at the performances conducted in most schools call for parents to be seated in rows while the performers, because of their small physical size, are placed up on the stage. For parents, what can sometimes make these events so fraught is that at this public moment they cannot do anything to help or support their child. (Indeed, these are probably the same emotions that can drive hockey parents to extreme acts.) But, as Schnoor notes, in these two events at DJDS, parents are by no means passive observers. They engage in the conventional outlets of cheering and clapping, but, less conventionally, at the Chanukah event they are performers too, and at the graduation ceremony they end up dancing with their children. Given what we have observed of the presence of parents in the life of the school, it is fitting that they are so actively involved here. What perhaps is more poignant is that, for a group of adults who often articulate a sense of alienation from organized Jewish life and the public performance of Judaism, these occasions involve them in experimenting in new behaviors, doing things publicly they may never have imagined they would do. To this extent the events' power comes from the blurring of boundaries between performers and audience and between the expression of old and new identities.

Children: At the core of what schools promise parents is the possibility of touching a different future for their children and themselves. Thus even in the most challenging educational environments parents can experience the sense of pure potentiality associated with the early years of childhood when they visit their children's school. When schools successfully embody a sense that the world is somehow different inside their walls, they invite an encounter with the ultimate questions of life, encouraging parents to wonder what their child might become. For Jews, vividly described by Simon Rawidowicz (1986) as an ever-dying people, a minority doubtful of its own survival, such ultimate questions can feel even more acute when one visits a Jewish elementary school. Parents can find themselves wondering whether things will be different for this group of children, whether they will find it less complicated to be Jewish, less difficult to juggle integration and survival.

These aspects of the environment mean that the events described here operate at an existential pitch experienced in few other settings frequented by parents. The context is already thick with meaning, much as it is in hospital delivery rooms and cemeteries. When the events at school are conducted with authenticity and spontaneity, as is so patently the case here, they enable Jewish parents to confront questions of rare personal importance. In these instances, they gain an intimation of the ultimate that few of them report finding in the synagogue.

The combined force of the elements identified here in making the school a site of religious and spiritual inspiration can be helpfully captured by a metaphor derived from Celtic folk religion, incongruous as this may seem in a study of Jewish families and Jewish schools. In early Celtic thought, "thin places" were considered to be geographical locations where the boundaries between the past, the present, and the future have somehow worn thin. It was believed that these localities could afford a special glimpse through the thin veneer of time, allowing one to suddenly become vividly aware of a particular truth or an event that has not yet occurred. In these surprising, usually wild, places it was possible, unexpectedly, to glimpse the sacred. At first sight mundane, these settings, when encountered in unmediated fashion, made it possible to glimpse numinous truths.

Jewish day schools are far removed from Celtic Ireland, but in our experience these apparently mundane settings possess a similar capacity to provide visitors and participants with a sudden and unexpected sense of the ultimate. Concerned though schools frequently are with the minutiae of management and organization, time tabling and carpooling, these sites of teaching and learning, of meeting and celebration, provide access to moments of meaning and significance.

Broader Implications

The value of the DJDS case is that it displays in acute fashion what such moments might look like. It indicates how a Jewish day school can provide a sense of profound social fellowship as well as a promise of protection from alienation. This case shows how parents hope to (and can) learn new Jewish knowledge from involvement in their children's schools. It demonstrates also that day schools can be an important source of Jewish inspiration that may border on a form of religious or spiritual experience.

In a later chapter we explore whether these findings are replicated in other more conventional day-school environments and in different cultural settings. First we turn to one further, more intimate arena where parents' personal lives intersect with their children's school and where the consequences of this intersection seem no less significant in the development of adult Jewish identities.

The School at Home

PRIVATE ENCOUNTERS
BETWEEN PARENTS AND
THEIR CHILDREN'S SCHOOL

The interaction between parents and schools occurs in two locations: at school itself, where parents come into direct contact with school life, and, less obviously, at home, where, through the mediation of their own children, parents encounter information, ideas, and practices that might not otherwise be part of their lives. It is too simplistic to talk about the impact of these encounters on parents' lives, because that inappropriately portrays parents as the passive recipients of a unidirectional set of influences from the school, but, just as we established in the previous chapter that DJDS takes on a significant role in the intellectual, social, and spiritual lives of parents when they come on to the school's premises, so in this chapter we explore how the school also possesses significance as a resource that informs the development of adult Jewish lives within the home.

Our interest in the school's role within the home does not mean that we have ignored more than four decades of sociological research demonstrating that schools are generally weak socializing agents, at least when it comes to their impact on children's lives (e.g., Central Advisory Committee for Education 1967; Coleman et al. 1966). Nevertheless we are encouraged by an emerging strand of thought within the sociological study of contemporary Jewry emphasizing the fluidity of adult Jewish identities to see if and how parents draw on what their children bring home from school in order to talk and act in new ways as adult Jews (Grant et al. 2004; Horowitz 2000). The combined impact of these two sociological trends cautions against expecting schools to have a clear and unambiguous impact on homes and suggests instead the need to probe the extent to which adults (parents), as active constructors of their own identities, adopt, adapt, or reject new experiences and encounters that their children bring from their schools into their homes.

Horowitz (2000) has written evocatively of adult Jews today as being on a journey that, in contrast to Jewish journeys of previous centuries, is largely internal: "The term 'journey' encompasses how Jewishness unfolds and gets shaped by different experiences and encounters in a person's life. Each new context or life-stage brings with it new possibilities. A person's Jewishness can wax, wane and change in emphasis. It is responsive to social relationships, historical experiences and personal events" (viii).

In this chapter we see whether what enters parents' homes from their children's school is sufficiently meaningful to provoke changes in parents' unfolding Jewishness. We explore if and how parents are responsive to the Jewish stimuli their children bring home from school and why some parents are more receptive to these stimuli than are others.

Data for this exploration come from two sources: first, from the parents we interviewed twice, when their children started at the school and again some two years later (whether or not they were still enrolled at DJDS), and second, from interviews with all the parents and children of one of the school's older grades. Taken together, these data enable us to piece together over time and over triangulated data points an account of what we call here "the school at home"—the encounters between parents and their children's school as they play out within the privacy of people's homes.

What Do Children Bring Home?

Unlike adolescents, who are notoriously reticent about reporting home what took place during school hours, younger children often need little prompting to share new knowledge or to involve their parents in celebrating their achievements and in confronting their problems. The nine-year-old students we interviewed found no difficulty in providing examples of how they taught their parents things that, in their words, their parents had either forgotten or had never known. Rose, a fifth grader, reports: "Every day when I go home I tell my mom and dad about what I do and they are like, okay, explain what you do. And sometimes they don't even remember what they did when they were in school, so I teach them and I help them remember what they did—like maths and spelling—because they did the same things as me."

Neither Rose's mother nor her mother's current partner were born Jewish (although her mother converted during her first marriage). Rose therefore teaches "them Hebrew because they don't exactly know Hebrew . . . and then when it's a holiday I just . . . teach them everything that we do. . . . Like on Chanukah, I tell them what you do and they just go like, oh, okay, I understand."

Joanne, who also "always likes to tell [her] mom and dad about all the different things that [she] learns," describes a similar pattern. She reports teaching her mother "how to do fractions" because "she'd forgotten how to do them," telling her parents about the exciting medieval times unit they're doing, and, she says, teaching her non-Jewish stepfather "prayers and stuff" because he doesn't know Hebrew.

It's striking that even one of Joanne's classmates, Isaac, has noticed how much Joanne's father has learned from the school:

Isaac: My friend Joanne, she's very nice. She has a dad that's not Jewish and she has a mom that is Jewish but her dad caught on very quickly to the Jewish religion.
DR: Why do you think he caught on to the Jewish religion?
Isaac: Well, because I guess he saw how they really celebrated a lot and he comes to the school a lot and I guess maybe he had a little bit of experience before he came into the family—it's her stepdad I think.

Based on what we hear from interviews with students, it is difficult to know how much of what children "teach" their parents is unsolicited and had been genuinely unknown or forgotten. Conversations with DJDS parents reveal, however, that because most of them did not experience an intensive Jewish education of their own, they do find themselves learning about Jewish holidays or concepts that they had not previously known. While all parents seem to have been familiar with the major Jewish holidays such as Rosh Hashanah, Yom Kippur, and Passover, many are surprised to learn from their children about Tu Bishvat (the new year for trees), Shavuot (the summer harvest festival), and other festivals that are not well known outside of Israel. As one father, Joe, who had attended Sunday school until his bar mitzvah put it, "[My daughter] knows more about some of the holidays than I do. I'm in big trouble . . . because I only know the top three." Even those who in their own childhoods experienced a more intensive Jewish education report learning from their children because of the more engaging educational approach employed by the school. Carrie Maybaum, a mother who received several years of Jewish educa-tion, explains how it is that she comes to learn from her son:

> What I find really nice about the school, I'm sure I'm not the first one to say it, is that the parents really learn so much from the kids. Listen, I do, and I have a very strong background, and still Daniel comes home and you know he'll sing me a new song or whatever or he'll tell me about *parashat hashavuah* [the Torah portion of the week]. Daniel was telling me that they did a little skit of the *parashah*. I know he'll never forget it and I will never forget it now. It's just great.

The most vivid and perhaps the most authentic instances of chil-dren bringing school into their homes occur less through the instruction of parents by children and more as a result of unex-pected and unsolicited outbursts of song and conversation with which children interrupt the regular life of the family. These out-bursts, less scripted than the child-parent instruction described earlier, take various forms. Children launch into blessings, con-temporary Hebrew songs, or traditional festival melodies in the car to and from school, at home when family are visiting, in the supermarket with parents, on the street, and at the beach. Some-times children surprise their parents with challenging theological questions that are stimulated by discussions at school, such as,

"If God is everywhere, so God is in the air, and I'm swallowing the air, so does that mean that God is in me and I'm God?"

The following story, told by Dina Funk, serves as a typical example of these interruptions even if her account is unusual in its elaboration and in the family context it describes, where both parents received a day-school education up to the seventh grade and where the family home is kosher.

> Dina: You see, Amos is really into the Jewish rituals.
> RS: Like what for example?
> Dina: Like singing *birkat hamazon*, like davening in the morning.
> RS: In the house here?
> Dina: Yeah and we don't. . . . So, we were on holiday and Amos comes in and says, "Mommy I want to lead the prayers today, it's the only way to welcome the new day." We go to the doctor's office; the song he's belting out is *birkat hamazon* [Grace after Meals], you know he loves it.
> RS: He is eating in the office?
> Dina: No, but he loves the song, and he knows it is supposed to be just after you eat, and he has taught me how to sing it as well. I mean it. I go to this WASPy little doctor's office and my kid is belting out *birkat hamazon*. I love it! And we have people over here on the weekend, his friends and their parents. And we are eating and then he stops everybody, "everybody, quiet, quiet, I want to say all the *brachot*," because we were having a snack. "And Mommy, can we say all of them?" Because in school what they do is they say all of them to cover all of the bases. . . . And so he wants to say all the *brachot*. He's into it.

How Do Parents React?

It is tempting to assume that if parents enroll their children at an all-day Jewish school they would expect if not desire them to acquire knowledge and develop behaviors of the kind described here. By now, however, it should be evident that no small number of DJDS parents came to the school feeling ambivalent about both the consequences of parochial education and their own Jewish identities. As a result, and as we see later, parents react to interruptions such as these in diverse and often unexpected ways. In broad terms these reactions can be viewed along a continuum from resistance and rejection on the one hand, to adoption and adaptation on the other. The first set of responses expresses an inclination to keep things the way they are and not to make changes in one's Jewish life; the second suggests a readiness to make changes in the home as a result of what children bring back from school.

Resistance/Rejection (Maintaining Equilibrium at Home)

Strictly speaking, the most extreme strategy available to parents for rejecting what children bring home is to withdraw them from the school altogether. Put differently, if parents feel so uncomfortable with the Jewish concepts and ideas their children encounter at school, they can transfer their children to other schools where they don't have to meet these problematic ideas and practices.

Having observed such patterns of reaction in other day-school communities, we assumed that a similar phenomenon was taking place at DJDS, particularly when during one year of our research as many as eight families transferred their children out of the school. However, once we interviewed four of these departees, we discovered that none of them attributed their departure to disappointment or discontent with the school's Jewish orientation. Their complaints were focused on other issues, such as the administration's lack of responsiveness to their concerns, disappointment at the school's academic quality, or social issues involving their children. These four families, at least, did not express through their departure a rejection of the Jewish content of what their children brought home.

That is not to say that all parents reacted positively to the ways in which their children were learning to talk and act Jewishly at DJDS. We already saw in the last chapter that when parents were troubled by what their children were learning they came to talk to Jessica Steinberg, the school's founding principal. She encouraged them to join the school's Religious and Education Policy Committee, where they could take up their concerns more systematically. In the following extract we see how one parent, Deborah Conway, who did indeed join the committee, described the situation that moved her to bring such concerns to the principal.

> Early on, it was around Yom Kippur, and Ben came home talking about how he was feeling guilty about something. He was worried that God was going to see what he was doing and how he was going to get punished, and God was writing down in a book whether you live or die. He had sort of got things misconstrued. I got really nervous and I wrote this letter asking how [the school was] dealing with this, how [they were] talking about God. . . . I don't want my kid to see God as this something out there watching and making sure what you do. . . . I wanted him to internalize right and wrong with his own kind of moral compass. I wanted that to be part of who he is, not because he was afraid that he's going to get punished. . . . So I wrote this letter to the school . . . and then I went in and we [talked] about how they deal with discussions around what God was and how Ben may have misinterpreted something that Joanna [the kindergarten teacher] said. . . . [In the end,] I felt confident that the school was not being really rigid about how they talked about these things . . . but I remember when I was at Talmud Torah and my Hebrew teacher told me, too, it was around the same thing, which is funny, that when you are walking to shul you should look behind you and if your shadow has no head you were going to die in the next year . . . and I was terrified.

In a later section we consider why a parent might, as in this instance, be inclined to take so seriously the theological language employed by her five-year-old child and not just dismiss it as childish talk. For the moment it is worth emphasizing that this reaction was not unique among parents, nor was the way it was prompted by concerns that derived from a parent's own problematic ("horrible," Deborah said) educational experiences as a child. We found that other parents complained to the principal for similar reasons, such as their children talking "too much" about God or about Israel, about their wanting to recite blessings "all the time," or simply because their children talked about theological matters in ways that made them feel uncomfortable.

An example of just such ambivalence was provided by Maytal Hillberg, a secular Israeli who had married a Torontonian and who as we saw in an earlier chapter was highly conflicted about not sending her children to the local public school. Maytal expressed profound discomfort with religious practices in general, and this unease came to a head when her daughter started to recite prayers at home that she'd learned at school. Like Deborah in the previous case, she managed to find a point of comfort that didn't require her to adjust her own thinking or practices. Instead she held onto the point of balance she'd found in terms of her own Jewish journey before her child started the school. She didn't embrace her child's new learning but found a way to compartmentalize it as something reasonable but that didn't relate to her own life.

> Maytal: In the beginning when all these prayers were new to Liat, she came home and would be singing her prayers. . . . She was singing *Adon Olam*, she was singing a bunch of prayers, like proper prayer, and I was standing here thinking I should write that school. "What are they sending my kid home with?!"
> Mike: I wasn't like that. I thought it was really cute. . . .
> Maytal: Like this was my initial reaction. It's like why are they teaching her that, and then I'm thinking, "Oh my God, I'm paying for this!"
> And then I came to the realization that it's good. I know all these songs. I know the tunes. I know the way they pray. Like I don't know the prayers. I don't know anything about prayers— I don't know what prayers you would say in the morning and what prayers you say before you eat. I didn't grow up with that. But she will know and it will make her richer and then she can choose. I don't care what she chooses, like it totally does not relate to me, these prayers. But then if she didn't go to this school she wouldn't have even known that they exist.

Neither Rejection nor Adaptation but Acceptance (Maintaining Equilibrium at Home)

One kind of parent reaction, also articulated by a very small number of interviewees, expressed a similar lack of change/responsiveness in reaction to what children brought home from school, but for profoundly different reasons. The three families who talked in this way explained that what children brought home made little difference to the Jewishness of their homes not because they weren't interested as such but because their children were getting from the school what they, the parents, would otherwise have given them or because it complemented the way they led their lives already. Carolyn Weinstein, the child of a non-Orthodox rabbi and in periods of her life an active synagogue member, elaborated on what this meant: "We are fairly educated for a liberal Jewish family, I would say. . . . I know that for a lot of people, what comes home [from school] with the kids is a major part of the Jewish thing that's going on in the house. . . . Whereas here, what comes home with Yoni just complements what's here already. I would say it's not more than what is here, it's just that now he gets to understand it more or be more part of it, you know what I mean?"

Talking with great self-awareness, Carolyn explained what this meant in terms of her own inner Jewish life and why "the school at home" makes little difference to her own sense of Jewishness: "I mean my Jewish identity actually is located in myself, and it may have its outlet in just everything I do. The decisions I make— what to eat, what to do on the holidays—all that revolves around me. My Jewish identity revolves around me, my home, my whatever. And a lot of it has an outlet in a synagogue context because Jews celebrate holidays in a synagogue community. I don't see that changing [because my child attends a Jewish day school]."

Adoption/Adaptation (Change at Home)

As we discover later, the kind of stability expressed by parents in these previously discussed cases (whether because of their engagement or because of lack of engagement with Judaism) was actually rare. More often than not, parents indicated that there had been significant change in their Jewish lives since or because their child had started at DJDS. Why this is so becomes apparent from parents' discussions about the changes in their homes, but we will wait until a later section of the chapter to spell out what we suggest are the motors behind these effects.

While in many instances parents talked vaguely about how "there would be no Jewishness in our lives if our child wasn't at the school" or that "there's now more Jewishness in this house than there's been for a long time," a small number of interviewees described precisely what this meant and how it happened. In chapter 2 we described at length the winding road to the school taken by Ed and Sharon Manning, an intermarried couple who only "checked out" DJDS because of "the sheer fact that Sharon's family was Jewish." In our second interview with the Mannings, after two years of association with the school, they described what had happened since. Ed, the non-Jewish partner in the marriage, takes up the story:

> Ed: When we first started [at the school] there was a lot of talk about [us having chosen a Jewish school].
> RS: You mean around the family?
> Ed: Yeah, and now I mean it's incorporated into our lives pretty easily to the point where it's not really noticed anymore. So on a day-to-day basis it's, let's see your Hebrew homework, let's see your regular homework, and we work through it. But then my mother-in-law, the other day, she is almost more surprised as to how it has affected me than Adam [our son] where now that he gets a challah every Friday and brings it home there's reason to do the Friday night prayers that we didn't normally do at all before. And while we've got challah and we made a covering for it so there's even more reason to do it. So I start pulling out the wine cup and the candles and my mother-in-law says, "Ed you're getting ready for Shabbat dinner!!" I said that's what we do now. And so most Fridays we say the prayers and incorporate it into our weekly life. It's something I look forward to but it's not like a special event anymore. It's a part of what we do.

The changes in their Jewish lives at home that other parents frequently describe have this quality: they are not dramatic and might not have been noticed if another person hadn't remarked on them. They don't necessarily involve taking on practices that were never previously observed by the family but rather entail doing them more frequently or more consistently as they become part of a routine organized around the rhythm of the school (or to be precise, the Jewish) calendar.

John, a father with some supplementary school Jewish education who married a woman who converted to Judaism at marriage, described a similar pattern:

> I wouldn't normally have Shabbat every Friday if Natalie was going to public school, and it's not that we wouldn't know how or we couldn't; it just probably would be easy enough to say, not this Friday! But she has it in school, she brings the challah home. How dare we not! Not out of fear, how dare we not, but of course . . .
>
> I have a role to play and that role therefore has brought more of that [Judaism] in to our home, because I think it would not be right of me not to.

For some parents it isn't even a question of performing practices more frequently but rather of doing them differently. Things now feel "different, more important," explains Ian Maybaum, someone who was enrolled in Jewish day school until the eighth grade but was turned off from Jewish life and ritual for several years. He reports: "I find that whenever I'm now in a family situation where it's Shabbat or a Shiva [a mourning house] or something, that I'm paying attention more, I'm reading along more. I find that I'm just more involved instead of standing at the back of the room, scratching my head waiting for this to end."

Ian's wife, Carrie, talks in more emotional terms about these effects. She helpfully points both to their son's role in this accelerating process and to its infusion of more Jewish spirit into the extended family. "I find that for me it's mostly his excitement about it and his interest and what he brings. You know Michael is at the age where everything Daniel [the DJDS student] does he imitates, so he has started to sing along too. He wants to help light the candle. It's the nice feeling you get, in fact it seems warm and fuzzy. And I can see it in my parents' eyes and my aunts and uncles' eyes, when you see them like that. . . . They haven't seen it in us since we were children."

Carrie's comments point to a phenomenon noted more explicitly by other interviewees that can best be described as a generational shift in the center of gravity of the family made possible by what children bring home from school. Children become drivers of Jewish life in place of their (frequently immigrant) grandparents. Of course, it might be argued that such a shift would have occurred whether or not children attended day school and that this change is simply part of a normal family cycle. But in at least one instance we found that this patently wasn't the case, because the same couple's oldest child did not attend a day school and hadn't prompted the family to take up Jewish practices as his younger brother was now doing. Although the older son "identifies himself as Jewish, he does so in a very sort of secular way." His younger brother, Graham, "because of what he's getting at a day school, wants to practice more at home. . . . We don't tend to do much at home, but we're getting pressure from Graham." And so, the parents explain, if formerly "the pace of Jewish life" in the family was set by their own parents, as their parents "do less and less, we . . . take on more and more." In this case, where one parent is an adult convert to Judaism, it seems that the engine of Jewish family life has skipped a generation from grandparents to grandchildren due to the interest and knowledge stimulated in the children by the school.

The intensification of Jewish life reported in all of these cases does not occur in uniform fashion, with parents taking up some script for Jewish living that their children have learned at school. Instead parents absorb and adapt what their children bring home within the family's existing culture and style—sometimes in ways that Jewish educators would find surprising if not challenging.

In a moving example, Charlotte, a mother whose ex-husband was Native and is herself Native-born but a Jew by choice, describes how her daughter introduced Hebrew into their home in ways that first seemed mundane but quickly assumed deep significance for her as a person wrestling with multiple identities. "Dina tries to translate names into Hebrew. If she has a friend, she asks what would that person's name be in Hebrew, or a dog or a cat. It's interesting. I lost a child. She was 4 1/2 months. I was carrying her for 4 1/2 months and I lost it. Her Native name was Wanaskaness. It means little flower, and Diana wanted to give her a Hebrew name. . . . [That's why] *we* named her Shoshana" (emphasis added).

No less vivid, but of a different tone, is the story told by the Lombards, among the founding parents of the school, in which they describe the interaction between Jewish concepts their children have learned at school and the nontraditional Jewish life of their own family. They describe a fluid process that flows to and from school, fueled, they indicate, by the kids' enthusiasm for their learning, which in turn, we suggest, finds a receptive audience at home.

> RS: So, has the school brought a lot of Jewishness to you guys as adults? . . . Has it really been a source of Jewish identity for you?
>
> Estelle: Well, it has for me. Well, [the kids] get excited about this stuff and so you can't help but sort of get caught up in it to a certain extent. And also you feel like you should, I mean if they are learning the stuff at school. Like when we went out for Chinese food on a Friday night, remember? And Lara goes, as we were leaving the restaurant, . . . "Isn't it Shabbat?!" . . . Or the time when Joshua was in SK [senior kindergarten] and every Friday they either say, or they have the parent write, what their mitzvah of the week is. So there we were having our Chinese food, eating, and there wasn't any shrimp left and Lara wanted another one, and Joshua said I could give her mine. Hey that could be my mitzvah! I don't think he did write it.
>
> Ray: I thought he did. I think we were talking about what if he did want to write it, would we feel comfortable enough at school . . .
>
> Estelle: You know what's great, like I remember in SK, Joanna, the teacher, asked the kids what their favorite foods are and I think Lara said shrimp, so a note goes up on the board. Like, yeah, I don't know about other Jewish day schools. I don't know how that would have gone over but I think . . . that's the reflection of the school and the families that go to the school.
>
> Ray: And for us not to feel guilty about it. I mean that's how we are living our life.

This last case is instructive. At first glance it might be taken to provide an example of parents unmoved by what their children bring home. After all, the family doesn't seem to have taken on any special Shabbat or dietary practices as a result of what their children have learned (like some of the families previously described). And yet during the course of this conversation it becomes apparent how much Ray and Estelle, who themselves received a limited Jewish education, have absorbed concepts and ideas from their children, if on their own terms. Their conversation is peppered with Jewish ideas and words, many of which they learned from their children and which they didn't know beforehand. Their social life is more or less built around the Jewish families they met through their children and who they didn't know before connecting with the school. They have also now joined a synagogue because, as they put it, "We thought, well, if our kids are going to a Jewish school, it would also be nice if we belonged to a synagogue." And yet, as they say, they are perfectly comfortable with how they lead their Jewish lives, shrimp and all. In their case, the school has not taken over the home, although it is undoubtedly in the home, brought there by their children, where it interacts and is snycretized with a preexisting family culture, as was the case with the interweaving of Native tradition and Hebrew language in the previous example of Charlotte, the Native-born mother.

Why Do Parents React in These Ways?

A Social-Psychological Account

It is tempting to attribute the general interest of DJDS families in (the Jewish content of) what their children bring home to a social-psychological profile shared by the great majority of parents in the school. From this perspective, DJDS parents can be characterized as "seekers" and "pioneers"; they were ready to sign up their children for an alternative school and did not simply choose the more convenient or conventional option of their local school. Half of our interview sample registered their children when the school had been in existence for fewer than three years and had no real track record. Evidently they are not resistant to experimenting with new experiences. The parent body seems also to be made up of people prepared to make major life changes at different moments in their lives. At least one partner in more than half of the twenty-eight couples we interviewed had either changed religion or marriage partner. Four members of the sample had changed both their marital and religious status. In terms of their religious behavior, the parents tend to be nonconformists who are certainly not inclined to do things because they or their own parents had always done them that way. Instead they develop their own rituals, often within their own family units. As we saw in an earlier chapter, they personalize their own religious practices on festivals and on the Shabbat. As one father, Dave Wallace, put it, "I never considered it worth paying to pray [at a synagogue]. . . . I could certainly do fine on my own." For another parent, lack of religious conformism came from "not liking to do things in a box . . . but preferring to do things his own way."

To return to the terms Horowitz (2000) used in her study of contemporary Jewish identity, there are strong grounds for conceiving of these families as composed of parents whose Jewish identities have waxed and waned over the life course. Their biographies are generally suggestive of people whose Jewishness has never been stable and rarely intensive and who, as a result of sending their child to a Jewish day school, seem now to be on a journey of intensifying Jewish involvement or at least on an interior journey where their subjective value commitments are intensifying while their religious and communal practices remain low.

Unfortunately, there are several problems with taking up this interpretative approach, at least in terms of applying Horowitz's categories to our data. First, it confuses cause with effect because it is not clear from our interviews and observations to what extent a particular individual's journey is stimulated by their choice of school and what the child brings home thereafter, or how much school choice and changes in the home are consequences of a journey stimulated by some other independent factor, such as the transition to parenthood. Second, this sociopsychological explanation infers motives for changed practices in the home from the behavioral characteristics of individuals (their school choice, their synagogue attendance, and their marriage patterns) without paying close attention to the reasons these individuals give for their own responses to their children. Finally, this explanation sets up the DJDS families as an outlier group (a minority among a minority in Horowitz's model) who differ in numerous ways from most other Jewish day-school families. In fact, as we see in the next chapter, when we compare the DJDS sample with other samples of day-school families they actually seem to share much in common with many of them.

For all of these reasons, we prefer to take up some more generalizable sociological categories to explain why people react as they do to the school in the home. These categories focus on the social and cultural circumstances evident in how people talk about their situations and depend less on the inference of internal motivations. The categories we have in mind—those of social capital and cultural capital—have been widely used for making sense of the relationships between parents and schools (Coleman and Hoffer 1987; Fine 1993; Lareau 2000; McNeal 1999) and can help provide a general explanation for the patterns we observe here even if they don't promise to provide reasons for the actions of particular individuals.

A Conventional Sociological Account

Social capital, as defined by Putnam (2000), refers to the "social networks among individuals . . . and the norms of reciprocity and trustworthiness that arise from them." Cultural capital refers to forms of knowledge, skill, education, and any cultural advantages a person has that give them a higher status in society (Bourdieu 1986). In the DJDS sample we find that, in almost all cases, those who are most inclined to adopt and adapt the Jewish content of what their children bring home from school are the families with limited Jewish social capital and limited Jewish cultural capital. Characteristically, when these families first enrolled at the school they had few Jewish friends and associates, only about half of them were connected with any other public Jewish institutions, and in many cases, because of the high number of conversionary or intermarried couples, they possessed attenuated Jewish family connections. These are the characteristics of limited Jewish social capital. As we have also seen, none in our sample had attended an all-day Jewish school outside Israel beyond the elementary level, and most had received a highly rudimentary Jewish education for between one and three afternoons a week until the age of twelve or thirteen. Their knowledge of Jewish literature, practice, and culture is limited, and few know Hebrew well. In short, they possess limited Jewish cultural capital.

It seems that once such families had made the decision to join the school, they took the most active advantage of opportunities to develop their own Jewish social and cultural capital. Counterintuitively, perhaps, families with the most limited preexisting Jewish cultural literacy and social life were those most ready to engage with the school at home. In fact, some made it clear (as we saw in chapter 2) that it was precisely because of their awareness of their own Jewish deficits that they chose the school in the first place. Others may not have enrolled at the school so deliberately, but over time they recognized the difference made in their lives both by their children's bringing their Jewish learning home from school and by their own participation as adults in the life of the institution.

Few articulated their social and cultural purposes, and in turn the impact of the school in their home, as well as the Spencers. They are a conversionary couple who had lived outside the city for most of their lives with no Jewish family and very few Jewish friends in Toronto. Today they live in a neighborhood where there are so few other Jewish families that "there is nothing other than us to support what Natalie learns at school." In the words of Barb Spencer, who converted to Judaism when she and her husband married nine years before,

> We are sort of like this: stand-alone, no culture, no family. So we are hoping that by sending our kids to Jewish day school that they'll come and teach us. And we are sort of there for each other as far as our Judaism and what we're doing. . . . If we weren't sending Natalie to a Jewish day school and were living in this neighborhood in Toronto, there would be no Jewishness in our lives. . . . We wouldn't normally have Shabbat every Friday . . . we wouldn't be planning to build a Sukkah in the backyard.

In the home of Adele and Dave Wallace, where Adele was highly informed about Judaism but never wanted to convert, the couple talk in very similar terms about originally choosing the school because Adele recognized that unless their son was in a Jewish school he would not develop a meaningful Jewish identity at home. (Dave was the person who had said that he couldn't see the point of

paying an institution to allow you to pray.) And having been connected to the school for more than four years, they can see the difference in their lives at home.

> RS: What is your Jewish family life like here, the three of you?
> Dave: Well, what are the components of it? We often will
> light the candles on Friday night and say Kiddush and because
> of Sam being at the school I think this leads us to celebrate the
> holidays in a more, not rigorous, but I guess more routine way
> because when holidays come up Sam is involved with them in
> school all the time. Since Sam was, I don't know how long
> now—since he was six or something like that, we joined a
> group, the Danforth Jewish Circle. Have you heard of it?
> RS: Yeah.
> Dave: And we do go to services on Yom Kippur and Rosh
> Hashanah. What else, dear?
> Adele: I would say that apart from the school . . . you see, we
> have very little close family. Dave has two cousins in town so
> they celebrate Jewish holidays. And his mom is 91. His father
> has passed away. His brother lives in Vancouver, and he isn't
> Jewish at all, so we have virtually no Jewish support struc-
> ture. . . . We do go to Montreal [where his mother lives] but it's
> kind of too late. His mom is 91, and in her 80s she didn't want
> us there for the holidays, it was just too much to handle, so I
> would say we have virtually no family Jewish culture except for
> what *we've* brought in since *he* has come to this school [empha-
> sis added]. The sorts of things that you mentioned and going to
> shul and so on. You've always davened on your own on the high
> holidays even before Sam. But the school was a pivotal decision
> for us because I kind of said to Dave I'm not prepared to do extra
> curricular Judaism, after school Judaism like an add-on. Like I
> felt if we were going to introduce him to a Jewish identity it had
> to be done authentically and in the context of a community
> because we had no family context for it—virtually none, I
> couldn't convey much.

Strikingly, in this case, it is Adele, the non-Jewish partner, who
was most alert to the Jewish cultural deficit in the home, a phenomenon replicated in Prell's (2007) study of intermarried families in Philadelphia. Adele's initiative (an ultimatum, in fact, as

she threatened to raise the child in her own faith if they didn't
register at a day school) combined with Sam's enthusiasm for
what he'd learned at school has stimulated a significant change in
the family's Jewish culture. This change, as we have emphasized
throughout this chapter, has not simply meant adopting what
comes home from school but rather adapting and integrating it
with what the parents themselves bring in. This is confirmed by
our conversations with Sam, who made the point that although
he was Jewish, because his father "comes from a Jewish family,
and his mother doesn't," they celebrate Christmas and Easter at
home. This is in contrast to some of his schoolmates' families,
who only celebrate Jewish holidays because in those families
"they're all Jewish."

In the last chapter we highlighted the extent to which parents
developed a sense of community and fellowship from their participation in the life of the school. Here we return to this theme only
to emphasize that those for whom the social aspect of school life
was most meaningful were the individuals and families who
came to the school with the most attenuated Jewish social capital. Weak Jewish social capital, it seems, is a predicate for active
participation in the symbolic frame of school life whether through
participation in school events that mark Jewish festivals or
though gathering together with other DJDS families in their own
homes to celebrate festivals together.

Joyce Silver provides an account of this dynamic and of how
intimately connected are the workings of social and cultural capital. Although Joyce was born into a traditional Jewish home, she
"went off the rails" following her parents' divorce, dropping out
of school and leaving home as early as was legally possible. Even-
tually she put herself through school and became a successful
businessperson. She maintained very few Jewish friends or family
relationships, but, in her own words, she "missed the connection
to the tradition, the stories and the songs and the really wonderful memories of my childhood in the religion." As a result of a
chance conversation, she "kind of fell into the DJDS . . . and it fit,
because I felt like in a sense that it was a school for the freaks—
the Jewish downtown freak parents. So it was perfect for me."

Retrospectively, this sense of belonging, of connection with a group of like-minded parents, is a large part of what Joyce has taken from the experience.

> I got a lot out of the school as a community. . . . My family is small. There's Joanne and the dog, myself and the hamsters, and the fish. So Joanne doesn't have cousins. I don't have a husband. Her father lives in Halifax, so [the school] really acts as an extension to the family. . . . And although I have become a bit concerned about the quality of the education, and that I now have to pay about $100 a week on tutoring in addition to my tuition at the school . . . it's the community that holds me there.

As Joyce reflects on what the school has meant to her, it becomes apparent that the school's significance goes beyond its nurturing of her social connection with other Jews. The school's importance derives also from what has been made possible in the home where she and her daughter together engage in what we called in chapter 3 the subatomic work of Jewish cultural construction, and what we can call here the cultivation of Jewish cultural capital. In many ways, and despite Joyce's self-description, this cultural work looks much less freakish and much more conventional than many of the previously described cases:

> So you know what, my home life now is very much talking about all the things that I had when I was a kid. We cook the same food and we build the Sukkah out here. We don't do it the kosher way but we do it and have fun; and Joanne, I'm thrilled that she knows. Like we lit candles on Friday night and her friend Cheryl was over and they did the long blessing over the wine which I don't know. I mean I can hum along with it but I never really learned it and it gives me great joy that Joanne knows the blessings. That's where she excels. She loves the study of the Torah and loves the prayers, so it's wonderful. I get such joy out of it. We talk a lot about that—about relationships to God. And I believe in God, it's in my own kind of Jewish-Buddhist way, but it's there. So I bring that into our home.

In many ways it is hard to imagine a more effective articulation of this chapter's themes than is provided by this statement. The school at home is a source for both Jewish social and cultural capital. Through their children and at private, often deeply meaningful moments, parents acquire new Jewish social connections and new Jewish knowledge. But, as we have repeatedly seen, social and cultural capital is not simply deposited at home by children returning from school. Parents process, adapt, and ultimately syncretize capital with and within an already existing family culture, and as we have suggested, this can take place in ways that Jewish educators might find challenging or at least idiosyncratic.

What Are the Consequences and What Is the Significance of These Reactions?

As we move toward considering the general implications of our findings at DJDS, it becomes important to ask how unusual are the cases described here. Are these the responses of "Jewish freak parents" who find themselves connected to Jewish day schools despite (and sometimes because of) their limited Jewish social and cultural capital? Or do the educational choices and involvements of these parents and their responses to the school both "as shul" and "at home" bear some resemblance to the behaviors of day-school families in other social contexts? These are the important questions to which we now turn.

Beyond Downtown
to the Suburbs

TESTING THE LIMITS
OF THE DJDS CASE

Taken together, the findings presented in chapters 2–5 reveal that, for many if not most parents at DJDS, choosing and sending their child to a Jewish day school possesses significance for their own lives as Jewish adults. In each of the last four chapters we found and described evidence of this significance: in parents' journeys to the school (an institution they chose for reasons that went beyond the quality of its educational program to factors in their own lives); in their modes of involvement within the institution, particularly within the cultural frame of school life or what we called the "school as shul"; and in their responsiveness to the knowledge their children brought home from school.

In this chapter we seek to account for these findings. We pose the kind of question that can be asked of all descriptive case studies that straddle a line between general phenomena and particular circumstances. We ask to what extent the relationships between parents and the school can be attributed either to a general tendency among Jewish parents today to find personal/religious meaning in their relationships with their child's (Jewish) school or to particular factors at DJDS that have produced the outcomes we observed. To state this more fully, we want to know whether the school's importance in the lives of parents is a consequence of phenomena such as the privatization of religious life and the inward turn of lived religion identified by sociologists of religion and by scholars of contemporary Jewry, or whether, alternatively, it can be more readily attributed to special features in this case, such as the school's smallness, its newness, or the religious non-conformism and non-Orthodoxy of parents.

Although it is not possible to confirm the existence of general social tendencies on the basis of one case study (or even by comparing findings from across a limited number of studies [Stake 1995]), it is possible to strengthen a hypothesis that such tendencies are at work if we can discount the possibility that phenomena observed within a single case occurred only as a result of circumstances particular to the case. To adapt an insight of Flyvbjerg's (2006), while case studies are weak devices in the construction of theory, they are powerful tools for falsification. Thus, if we can determine that outcomes similar to those observed at DJDS do occur in circumstances that are significantly different from it, we can at least disprove the notion that such outcomes only occur in unusual schools such as DJDS with groups of parents peculiarly like those found there.

In order to advance this research goal, we present data in this chapter from settings where schools and their parent bodies are identifiably different from those at DJDS. We draw on this data in an attempt to interrogate the following set of claims that might be made about the effect of the particular circumstances at DJDS on the adult Jewish identities of its parent body: (1) that it is only because DJDS is a small school (with fewer than seventy families) that parents are so much connected to one another and to the institution and its mission, (2) that it is only because DJDS is a new school (less than eight years old) that parents are so heavily involved in and inspired by its programs, and (3) that it is only because DJDS parents come to the school with such limited Jewish social and cultural capital that they are so much affected by their involvement in school life and are responsive to the Jewish content of what the school teaches their children.

To interrogate these claims we take up data collected from six other day schools, each of which differs in significant ways from DJDS. The essential features of these six schools were described in chapter 1, but we reintroduce them here.

1. *Rav Kook School*: K–8; 540 students; modern-Orthodox day school; founded in the 1980s; located outside the municipal boundaries of Toronto in one of the most densely populated Jewish neighborhoods in Ontario.
2. *Ben Gurion School*: K–8; 850 students; secular Jewish day school; founded in the 1960s; situated in a wealthy Toronto neighborhood where some of Canada's best-known synagogues can be found.
3. *Hirsch Academy*: K–8; 250 students; founded in the 1940s under Orthodox Jewish auspices to serve students from across the community; located on the edge of a business park in suburban Centreville midway between the school's two main feeder congregations.
4. *Frankel School*: K–8; 230 students; launched during the early 1980s under the auspices of the Conservative Solomon Schechter day school network; located in purpose-built premises with ample grounds in one of Centreville County's most prestigious school districts.
5. *Hafetz Haim Prep*: K–8; 200 students; ultra-Orthodox, non-coeducational school for boys and girls launched in the later 1980s by a group of parents who split away from the Hirsch Academy; located in an area of longtime Jewish settlement on two sites, each modified for use as a school.
6. *Leo Baeck Academy*: K–4; 60 students; Reform day school founded in the 1990s with help of matching funds from a private national Jewish foundation; renting space from one of the oldest suburban Reform temples in Centreville.

The ways each school differs from DJDS are summarized in table 6.1.

Taking up data from interviews conducted with more than one hundred parents whose children attended these schools, we will interrogate each of the three claims stated earlier.

Claim 1: It is only because DJDS is a small school (with fewer than seventy families) that parents are so much connected to one another and to the institution and its mission.

Table 6.1   Comparison of Sample Schools

		School			Parents	
		Denominational orientation	Small (fewer than seventy families)	New (less than eight years old)	Limited Jewish social and cultural capital	Canadian
Toronto	DJDS	Religiously pluralistic/ community	√	√	√	√
	Ben Gurion	Nonreligious/ community	X	X	X-√	√
	Rav Kook	Modern-Orthodox	X	X	X	√
Centreville	Hirsch	Modern-Orthodox	X	X	X	X
	Frankel	Conservative	X	X	X-√	X
	Hafetz Haim	Ultra-orthodox	√	X	X-√	X
	Leo Baeck	Reform	√	√	√	X

√ = presence of identified factor   X = absence of identified factor

Advocates for small schools argue that, unlike big schools where so much effort is expended on the maintenance of efficient educational bureaucracies, in small schools students are at the center of the educational enterprise where they "possess a sense of visibility, of significance, and the hope to negotiate the tricky terrain of identity" (Ayers 2000, 5). Advocates claim that parents also play a different role in these places. In small schools "parents are not annoying outsiders to be tolerated, nor phony 'partners.' . . . [They] must be gift and asset, and often decision-makers regarding broad policy and direction" (5).

At DJDS, where each year all of the new parents and their "buddies" can sit together in a single comfortable circle and where the board's standing committees seem always in need of an infusion of new members to continue functioning, the school's

small size fosters a high degree of social cohesion and social interaction among adults as well as children. Of course, parents don't
suddenly abandon long-standing social networks once their children join the school; but they are invited and pushed to develop
social and working relationships with the parents of their children's peers such that by the time their children have been in the
school for a number of years, it is no surprise to hear parents say,
as Ray and Estelle Lombard did, that their "friendship base and
community really is at the school."

A similar effect seems to be at work at the Leo Baeck Academy
in Centreville, a school with just forty families at the time of our
research. With so few families on which to rely to run a full range
of extra-curricular and regular schooltime activities, parents report
having to do almost everything from stuffing envelopes to planning
the annual gala to ferrying children on school trips. Despite the
sense of fatigue their efforts produce, they nevertheless recognize
that by working so closely with other parents during many hours of
joint volunteer work they have developed valuable friendships
with people they didn't know previously, "people who want their
kids to be raised in the same way we want our own kids to be
raised." As one mother explained: "I would say that, now, 99 percent of our friends and our social life involves other parents from
LBA. I mean we knew some of those people, perhaps half of them,
before we started, from our temple. But we didn't know them very
well until we started LBA. Now they've become very close friends.
Those are the ones we socialize with" (Vivienne Levy).

Such relationships, although characteristic of parent life in
small schools, are by no means absent from the larger schools in
our sample, even where bureaucracies have indeed developed to
take on some of the responsibilities otherwise shouldered by volunteers. It is true that in the larger schools (those, e.g., with more
than 120 families) parents can afford to be more selective about
how they get involved because they know that other parents or
professionals are available to take their place. Nevertheless,
intense and meaningful social interaction—what some call a feeling of community—is no more the monopoly of small schools
than is parental passivity and alienation exclusively associated
with larger schools.

In Centreville, for example, some of the families who spoke most eloquently about how their social lives had taken shape around their school involvements were from the Frankel School, an institution with more than 230 children, and, at the time of this research, the second largest day school in the city. At Frankel, many parents have become particularly close with the cohorts of families with whom they entered the school, causing one mother to state, "You always become friends with the parents of your kids' friends," even though our research indicates that in many instances parents' social lives do not actually revolve around their child's school. By way of contrast, at Hafetz Haim, the school with the second smallest number of families in our sample, the parent body is so little involved as volunteers that in some years the school struggles to find enough parents to run a PTA. There are a host of complicated reasons for the situation at Hafetz Haim (the school includes a high proportion of faculty with their own children in the school and also a high number of families with more than a half-dozen children), but the point is that parental involvement is not necessarily correlated to the size of a school, nor is parents' sense of connection to other parents and to the institution's mission and values. We can therefore state with some certainty that the smallness of DJDS should not be seen as an incubator of relationships that would not otherwise occur in larger, more conventional day-school environments, as day schools, in general, are rarely larger than medium-sized public schools. If DJDS parents do find so much meaning in and around their children's school, it does not seem to have been a special consequence of the school's size.

Claim 2: It is only because DJDS is a new school (less than eight years old) that parents are so heavily involved in and inspired by its programs.

If size isn't everything, then many say that youth is. As we reported in an earlier chapter, when we have shared data from DJDS with colleagues, they have told us that the intensity and investment we observed at the school was a special consequence of its newness. In older, more established institutions, we've been told, one doesn't find parents so willing to devote their time to everyday school matters or so excited about commonplace features of school life.

Earlier we wrote about how a vein of utopianism runs through the discourse of many parents when they speak about DJDS. They frequently talk as though the school is possessed of unlimited potential, sometimes with complete disregard for mundane factors such as staff turnover and budgetary constraints. As we have already suggested, it is possible that this is how people typically imagine newly launched schools, where there seem to be few limitations on what they promise. In these circumstances parents exist in what Victor Turner calls a state of *communitas*, a special feeling of connectedness that occurs at instants of pure potentiality and of cultural creativity (1982, 44). For Turner, *communitas* is a liminal condition, characteristic of utopian projects; it exists in a "kind of institutional capsule or pocket which contains the germ of future social developments, of societal change" (45). In his terms, this is usually a temporary state that calls for and provides a deep sense of investment and a heightened sense of belonging, much as we have seen in the behaviors and talk of DJDS parents who have invested themselves in a model of Jewish education and community that differs significantly from the local norm.

Again, the other school in our sample where Turner's description is most apt is the Leo Baeck Academy of Centreville, a Reform Jewish day school founded four years before we started our research. As at DJDS, Leo Baeck parents seem inspired by both the fragility and the possibility of their new school. They recognize that the precariousness of the school's financial situation "requires" them to make available to the school, over many hours a week, their skills in marketing, real estate, arts and crafts, and organizational matters. Their contribution can make a discernable difference to the quality of life in the school (to the benefit of their own children) during a start-up phase when the school's financial situation is so insecure from one year to the next. They also believe that their contribution can affect the institution's long-term viability (to the benefit of other children), and it is in this latter respect that they articulate a sense of the school's potential to contribute to what one parent called the "bigger picture . . . the survival of Judaism in America." As this parent explained, in a city where the majority of Jews are affiliated with Reform synagogues, a Reform Jewish day school "really speaks to a lot of people . . . making it possible for Judaism to flourish in America after several generations of assimilation." As another parent grandly expressed it, "This school is preparing the next generation of the community's leaders."

While it is easy to understand why new schools engender such a heady mix of concern and expectation among parents, it does not mean that more established institutions are incapable of stimulating similarly powerful emotions. We found that other schools in our sample inspired parents to devote themselves just as intensively to their children's education either when parents felt a deep sense of identification with the mission and values of the institution or when parents were connected to the school through a multigenerational association as graduates or as the children of graduates.

The Hirsch Academy in Centreville is the oldest school in our sample, having been founded during World War II when there were few Jewish day schools beyond the eastern seaboard of the United States. It is the largest day school in Centreville, with about 250 children enrolled. In our interviews with a sample of parents from the school we found few, if any, who talked in idealistic or utopian fashion about their hopes or experience of the school. (To that extent the institution had long ago evolved from what Max Weber would call a charismatic to a bureaucratic phase.) But there are many who expressed a deep sense of identification with the school's values and religious ideology as well as a feeling of fellowship with other Hirsch families. When one father talked about his relationship to the school, he used language that resonated with Turner's depiction of the blurring of identities and boundaries at liminal moments within the life of an institution, but in this case the parent was describing an association that stretched over eleven years.

> We weren't going to send our kids anywhere else because this is where our values are reflected. . . . So even if we have personal disagreements with how the school is sometimes, and we have our disagreements with teachers . . . we're not going to start

shopping around [for another school]. . . . This is the only game in town for people like us. . . . We want this mixture of secular and religious studies, and Zionism, and the right type of families who are shomer Shabbat and shomer kashrut [observe the Sabbath and keep kosher]. . . . This is who we are! (Charles Caplin)

Another Hirsch parent described a relationship with the school that extended over more than twenty-five years. He attended the school as a student until the ninth grade, he had a ten-year-old daughter who'd been in the school since kindergarten, his wife was now teaching in the school, and over the course of eight years he had been involved in numerous committees on which he had represented the school within the wider community. While he didn't think that the school had prompted any changes in his own Jewish life as an adult, because "that's the way we were already living as a family," it is striking that he remembers his own parents becoming "more observant . . . keeping kosher in and out of the house . . . observing Shabbat" after he started at the school as a student and after his own parents and grandparents became board members.

As with many other Hirsch families, there is in his case an absence of clear boundaries between home and school because of so many personal and professional connections with the school spanning so many years. It seems that parents do not so much choose the school as exist within a social network where school, synagogue, and home connect seamlessly—"incestuously . . . in a positive way," in the words of one parent. For some this produces frustration that, in their opinion, there are no other school options available to them "given who they are." But, for most, this interweaving of school, home, and community provides the basis for a deep sense of loyalty and commitment to the school, no matter what its flaws.

These effects are quite different from those we observed among the families interviewed from the Rav Kook School in Toronto, an institution founded more recently but with a similar religious and educational orientation to that at Hirsch. At Rav Kook, parents were no less concerned about what they called the "fit" between the school and its families and the way they lead their own Jewish lives, but their careful selection of a school as congruent as possible with their own identities did not translate either into the kind of hyperactive involvement in school life that we saw at DJDS, Leo Baeck, and Hirsch or into the same blurring of boundaries between school and home.

At the heart of our inquiry is the question of how to account for these differences. It is possible that in the competitive day-school marketplace in Toronto, where there are three or four close alternatives to Rav Kook, many parents act much as consumers who discerningly (and dispassionately) pick a product in relation to a set of measures, such as the school's approach to Hebrew language, coeducation, and general studies, rather than looking for an institution—a social reality—with which their identities can merge. It is possible also that because the school is much more financially secure than DJDS, Leo Baeck, and even Hirsch (which despite its size draws from a highly conscribed pool of customers) parents can afford to stand back from fully investing themselves in the school's everyday life without risking its viability. What is more likely is that a large part of the difference between parental behaviors at these schools can be attributed less to the institutions themselves (their size and their age) than to the profile of the parents they serve. It is this possibility that brings us to the third claim that can be made about the specialness of the DJDS case.

Claim 3: It is only because DJDS parents come to the school with such limited Jewish social and cultural capital that they are so much affected by their involvement in school life and are responsive to the Jewish content of what the school teaches their children.

Historically, parents who chose to pay thousands of dollars each year to send their children to all-day Jewish schools were synagogue members and residents of Jewish neighborhoods and had been recipients of a relatively intensive Jewish education themselves. With few exceptions they were Jewish from birth, Orthodox in denominational orientation, and married to other Jews. Paying for all-day Jewish schooling constituted, therefore, the most complete expression of an intensely engaged Jewish identity (Ackerman 1969; Schiff 1974).

As will be evident by now, DJDS parents depart from these patterns in a variety of ways. Most do not have extensive Jewish family or social networks, about half are not members of synagogues, and many by their own admission experienced either a partial or unsatisfactory Jewish education during their formative years. These are the reasons why we characterized most of our DJDS interviewees as possessing limited Jewish social and cultural capital and why we claimed that their Jewish lives are so much interrupted by the encounter with their children's school. Having chosen a Jewish school for their child, they seem ready to explore opportunities to learn about Judaism, to experiment with the Jewish practices their children bring home, and to develop meaningful relationships with other adult Jews.

The different relationship between Rav Kook parents and their children's school can be readily attributed, then, to their possessing a more traditional day-school profile in which they are already connected to a multitude of other Jewish institutions and therefore possess already rich personal Jewish lives. This is something parents have no difficulty explaining. As one Rav Kook parent pithily summed it up, "The school is not there to help define my Jewishness per se," or in the words of another, "My Jewish identity has already been formed, I don't need the school to do that for me. I need it to do that for my daughter." As yet another parent explained, "You send your kids to a school where they are going to reinforce what you do. It's very clear that for me personally [the school] is not as important as shul where I go every day and not just once in a while."

Plainly, the parents quoted here were already in possession of extensive Jewish social and cultural capital when they chose their child's day school. They have therefore been little changed by what their child brings home, by their experience of school programs, or by their participation in school committees. In this respect, they are representative of the kinds of families who made up an overwhelming proportion of the day-school population during the first three-fourths of the twentieth century.

What is striking in our data, however, and what makes them so important as a barometer of change in contemporary Jewish society is that they not only confirm how far day-school families now depart from this traditional profile but they also underline that those who depart from this profile can be found in a very wide variety of schools (certainly within all six schools in our comparative sample). Without question, there are in non-Orthodox schools higher concentrations of parents with limited Jewish social and cultural capital and for whom this is their first significant engagement both with a Jewish institution and with large numbers of other adult Jews. Nevertheless, there is also a substantial minority of parents in Orthodox schools who in their own terms are *baalei teshuvah*, and who, in sociological language, are engaged in a process of intensifying Jewish engagement, often with little previous Jewish social or cultural exposure.

The following examples have been selected in order to establish as vividly as possible that the processes and phenomena (the involvement, personal investment, and personal growth of adults) we observed at DJDS can be found across the sample of six schools regardless of size, newness, viability, or denomination.

1. At Hafetz Haim Prep, one pair of interviewees were unusually frank in indicating the extent to which choosing a school for their child was shaped by an awareness of their own needs and goals. They had immigrated to the United States with Jewish backgrounds that varied between nominally and moderately affiliated and identified two key factors that attracted them to the school. First, and more conventionally, they desired to provide their children with an opportunity to experience the kind of intensive Jewish education they'd never had themselves and that they couldn't yet provide at home. Second, and more revealingly, they explained that they were inspired by the families they saw at Hafetz Haim, families who, in their own words, they "would like their own family to be like." They chose the school because they wanted to emulate the adult role models they found there.

2. A family at the Frankel School whose children had started out in public school described with great vividness how their Friday nights were changed over the years by what their children brought home from day school. In so doing they describe a process

that can best be characterized as the accumulation of Jewish social and cultural capital:

> Anna Seaton: Our Friday nights evolved as the kids got older. . . . We had a Friday night dinner, and they would bring in the prayers, the full Kiddush, and some of the singing and songs. It was easily ten, fifteen, twenty minutes prior to dinner, from what they had been doing in school. . . . It became that that was the night that we were home, nobody was going anywhere.
>
> John Seaton: And it also became social, that we were inviting a family over or we were going to a family's house. And it was always fun to see other people's traditions . . . and we would sort of incorporate what they were doing. . . . So it's just like we did a lot of learning from our children and from what they brought home from school and then sharing with other families from Frankel.

3. A mother at the Rav Kook School also described unanticipated changes that she and her husband had made to their personal religious practices since their child had started school. They had lived in Israel for a few years and had been quite secular. They had become more religious since moving to Canada and therefore looked for a day school that "would make it easier" to maintain some of the religious practices they'd taken on. The mother revealed that, originally, she had expected it would be more difficult to abide by the school's expectation that all women wear skirts on the school premises than it would be to maintain a kosher home. She admitted: "I started out keeping an emergency skirt in the car [in the event of being called to school at short notice], but then when it came to it, it seemed like such a strange thing to do. So then I said, I'll just wear a skirt to the school. But it was just too annoying to change three times a day, so now I've just got used to wearing skirts."

The father found that his dress habits changed too. He only began to wear a *kippah* (Jewish head covering) when his son started school because that was a norm observed by almost all Rav Kook fathers. Then, when their son had to wear tzitzit (ritual fringes), he "started wearing them too because, he said, it was unreasonable to say to their son that Jewish boys wear tzitzit but Jewish fathers don't."

4. A couple with a child at the Ben Gurion School described no less dramatic changes in their lives of a completely different kind since their child started school. The husband and wife were both born in South Africa, and when they settled in Toronto six years earlier they had bought a home in a downtown neighborhood close to Lake Ontario where there were few Jews. It was somewhere they felt so comfortable that, they say, they didn't go elsewhere in the city for weeks at a time, especially during the summers. They put their eldest child's name down at Ben Gurion as well as at four or five other schools. Ben Gurion, the father explained, reminded him of his much-loved day school in South Africa. But when the mother received a call from the school to tell her that their son had been admitted, she confesses, "I truthfully considered not telling [my husband] that he got the spot" because it would either mean a long commute across the city every day for their son or moving from their lakeside home.

In the end they accepted the place at Ben Gurion—"How could you not when there is so much competition?"—and moved to a much more visibly Jewish neighborhood to be closer to the school but not on top of it. "It meant selling our house, looking for a new house, and shifting communities. It feels like we have moved cities, like it's been a huge shift—I think it has been a huge move." Now, a year later, they are meeting people on the street who also have children in the school, and they are weighing up which of the area synagogues to join. Their lives, which, since leaving South Africa, had little Jewish social or religious content, now seem to be moving in a different direction, inspired largely by having enrolled their child in a day school.

5. A mother at the Leo Baeck Academy, who growing up had "felt very proud of her Jewish identity, just not in a practicing sense," and had married "a graduate of the best schools Catholic education had to offer," described her reaction to a special program in her child's school. Her words resonate with some of the most powerful responses we observed at DJDS:

I think that this has been the most significant Jewish experience in my life. . . . The other day the kids were up there and
they wrote their own siddurim. [The teachers] wrap them up [in
a Torah wimple] and each child had written a piece in their
Hebrew names and they sat in the middle of the room. And I
looked at them and I saw that continuing thread (whether or
not you believe in heaven or anything) of how the Jewish people could go on for 5,000 years. And in the room I saw the kids
that were going to take it to the next place. That is a beautiful
thing that I don't find in synagogues because they're so big, so
huge, so hurried; the program is so scripted. There are just
unimaginable moments of beauty that take place there that we
wouldn't get to see and judge as spiritual if we weren't a part of
it. (Greta Diamond)

6. Finally, a mother at the Hirsch Academy who described herself as having received a "minimal Jewish education" as a child
offered the following description of what takes place in the intimacy of her home when her daughter returns from school.
Tellingly, her narrative slips back and forth between an account
of her own learning and that of her daughter's:

I think that the most important thing for me is to be home with
my daughter when she comes home from school and helping
her with her homework and just learning *from* her [emphasis
added]. I'm learning to write cursive Hebrew. I never learned
cursive Hebrew. Now she knows block letters, and cursive
Hebrew and then next year it's a different alphabet, almost a
Romanaic alphabet that one of the commentators used, called
Rashi script. So she is going to learn that next year. It's different—it's a whole different alphabet. Just when you think you
got one down—I got the block letters down a couple years ago
now I'm teaching myself the cursive. So that's my connection
to the school that I really enjoy, it's that I'm learning along with
her. (Marjorie Pearlman)

As we have written elsewhere, the significance for this mother of
her interaction with her child's Jewish schooling is hard to exag-
gerate (Pomson 2007). At the end of her interview, when asked
whether there was anything she wanted to highlight, she said:

What I would like to say is: when my daughter comes home, when she studies the Chumash, she'll read from the Torah, and she'll be reading along in Hebrew and translating in English as she goes along—she is nine years old. And I just start crying. And she says mom you stop crying you know. I explain to her, I said to her, mommies cry when they are sad and when they are happy. And I said, I'm so happy that you have a Jewish education. You know all of this stuff. I had to learn this when I was much older.

One suspects that if all identifying features were removed from these accounts, it would be difficult to match these cases with particular schools. Many, if not all, of the families in these cases could even come directly from the DJDS parent body.

Such a conclusion is of no small consequence. First, it affirms an argument suggested by the DJDS study, that Jewish day schools generally play an important role in the personal and religious lives of Jewish adults. At the same time, these six additional cases indicate why DJDS parents have been unusually responsive to the Jewish content of their children's school. This is not because of the school's size or newness but because of a concentration of families in the school with limited Jewish social and cultural capital. Other schools, spanning the denominational spectrum, attract families with a similar profile and sometimes in large numbers, but the distinctive downtown location and particular educational orientation at DJDS have brought about a demographic concentration that makes the school such an unusual but by no means unique arena for the interaction between them and their children's Jewish education. This suggests a slight modification to the thesis with which we started this chapter: it seems likely that Jewish day schools do possess significance for the personal lives of parents but that those for whom they possess greatest significance are the parents who come to schools with limited prior Jewish social and cultural capital.

This may sound like a meaningless if not tautologous claim— that those who gain most from the encounter with day schools are those who have most to gain from it. Yet it is worth emphasizing how much this claim departs from previous assumptions about the relationship between non-Orthodox parents and Jewish day

schools. Since the 1970s, a spate of studies have found that less traditional families enrolled their children in day schools *in spite of*
the Jewish education they offered (Kapel 1972; Kelman 1979; Zeldin
1988). It was assumed that many parents were prepared to tolerate
the Jewishness of Jewish day schools as the price for access to the
kind of quality general education they provided. Even today this
continues to be an assumption widely held by those who market
day schools within the religiously non-Orthodox community
where the capacity of day schools to graduate Ivy League candidates
is emphasized rather than their potential to prepare students with
particular Jewish strengths (DAF 2006). Yet the cases briefly sur-
veyed here confirm what was suggested by the DJDS study: that a
lack of prior Jewish engagement does not necessarily inhibit parents' interest in a school's Jewish content or their responsiveness to
their children's Jewish learning; it may actually vitiate their interest and engagement in the school. This, we suggest in the next
chapter, is a conclusion of great significance for scholars of contemporary Jewry and for Jewish educators. It raises questions about
what kinds of venues are most likely to stimulate the Jewish journeys of Jewish adults. At the same time, it also calls for considering
what should be the response of day-school educators to the changing needs and interests of parent clients, many of whom were once
thought aloof toward the Jewishness of Jewish schools.

Postscript: Is DJDS a Canadian Phenomenon?

When we first sought publishers for this book, some American-
based editors told us that they were skeptical about the relevance
or application of a "Canadian" study such as ours to an American audience. Essentially we were told that the phenomena we
observed were quirky consequences of the Canadian context and
were unlikely to be replicated in the United States where families
like those we found at DJDS were unlikely to abandon a long-
standing loyalty to public education.

By now—with the selection of examples from the day schools
of Centreville—it should be clear that the differences between the
Canadian and American context are of limited significance when

it comes to parents' relationships with their children's Jewish school. Admittedly, Jewish families in Toronto are much less attracted to their local public schools than are their peers in Centreville, where the suburban public schools are regarded as among the best in the country. In Toronto, as well, because of the existence of a long-established publicly funded Catholic school system, parents have far fewer reservations about abandoning the shared civic space provided by public schools. But, as we have seen, there are plenty of families in Centreville who, despite little previous association with Jewish culture and society, find themselves drawn to the idea of sending their child to an all-day Jewish school. Sometimes this is despite having intentionally purchased homes in school districts where they could have access to the best public schools, and sometimes this is despite the long-standing belief, as one parent put it, that "someone who went to Jewish day school was a dork with a yarmulke."

As we have noted on a number of occasions, there are in fact great similarities between the context and character of DJDS and those of the Leo Baeck Academy in Centreville. Both schools contain a significant minority of intermarried or conversionary families. Both schools are organized around a progressive educational vision that distinguishes them from their immediate competitors in the public and Jewish systems. Both schools were even founded with start-up assistance from the same U.S.-based philanthropy. This does not mean that the schools are identical. Leo Baeck is affiliated with a particular religious denomination, whereas DJDS is determinedly nondenominational. Leo Baeck was founded by grandparents who were concerned that their grandchildren might not be or were no longer being raised as Jews; DJDS was launched by a group of parents who wanted to create a day school that would be open to the non-Jewish world beyond the school doors. At the time of our research, Leo Baeck was still being led by its founding principal; DJDS, over a slightly longer period, had seen a number of changes in the school's professional leadership. In these respects, the two schools have been shaped by the particular concerns of their founders and by the constraints and challenges in their local communities. But in making these comparisons it is evident that the two schools are more similar than they are different. Certainly it is not the case that one school is peculiarly Canadian and the other American, or that one is uniquely a downtown institution and the other distinctively suburban. More reasonably, the creation and operation of these two schools is indicative of changes in Jewish identity and society that go beyond the particulars of individual communities. Our research at both these schools suggests a need to reassess how Jewish adults construct meaning in their lives. These implications and the challenges they pose for Jewish educators are what we address in our conclusion.

Conclusion

LEARNING FROM
WHAT'S DOWNTOWN
Lessons from Sociology for Jewish Education

Almost all adults have been to school at some time in their lives. Some, as we have seen, seem to seize the opportunity to go to school again.

A review of the popular media and Internet postings suggests that this is a matter of parents no longer trusting teachers, of anxious parents refusing to let go of their children, and of parents taking their rights as consumers to unimagined and invasive extremes. Newspaper and magazines are replete with horror stories of "hovering parents," "aggressive advocates," or simply, and most patronizingly, "bad mothers." These stories all provide ample reason why, as one *Time* magazine article put it, "teachers hate parents" (Gibbs 2005).

Although this book has discussed parents who seize the opportunity to return to school, our study has not been an investigation of parental interference or of "typical, interfering Jewish parents," as one principal crudely put it to us. Doubtless, interfering parents do exist at DJDS, and their interference is probably part of the reason for the high turnover of senior professionals in the school. But early on in the research process at DJDS we decided not to conduct a study of the conflicts we observed between parents and teachers, or between school committees and the principal. Those conflicts are familiar phenomena in almost every school, and not just in private Jewish institutions, something depressingly suggested by the fact that a Google search of "parent + conflict + school" produces a yield of 11,800,000 items.

151

With this study we chose instead to pay attention to something we found more interesting, partly because we share a concern for the study and development of Jewish identity but also because we identified a phenomenon that surprised us and that seemed to surprise many parents and professionals with whom we spoke. Put simply, we found that children's schools—children's Jewish elementary schools, to be precise—play an important role in the lives of many Jewish adults.

A previously quoted comment from Ian Seigal, a DJDS parent, nicely communicates the unexpectedness of this phenomenon: "I'm pleasantly surprised by how much I like to talk about [my child's school]. I never thought it would be something like that. . . . You know, you send your child to school, that's what you do. It's part of being a parent. But it's more than that, and I realize that [now], and I definitely did not realize that before. . . . I didn't think as a parent it would be any different [from when I was student], but it does feel different. It's more important."

In this conclusion we argue that the unexpected relationships that parents develop with their children's Jewish day schools are best understood against the backdrop of changing patterns of Jewish identification over the last century, with adult Jews finding personal and religious meaning in a diversifying range of settings. In the final sections of this chapter we explore the implications of these changing patterns for teachers, principals, and community planners—Jewish professionals whose current responsibilities do not call for thinking of Jewish elementary schools as environments well suited to the nurture of adult Jewish engagement.

Changing Patterns of Jewish Identification

It is helpful to situate our work, as a study in the sociology of Jewish identity, within broader theoretical themes in the study of ethno-religious identity. As we have written elsewhere, recent reflections in this field point to an important shift in our understanding of how individuals construct their sense of ethnic or religious identity (Schnoor 2006).

Scholars of ethnic studies, for example, argue that ethnic identity is no longer a fixed, essentialist status but rather a social construction that is continually negotiated and renegotiated by the individual (Nagel 1994; Spector and Kitsuse 1987). Ethnic identifiers can now slip in and out of ethnic roles depending on the social context (Waters 1990).

Scholars of the sociology of religion have described a similar societal shift in religious identity construction. Robert Wuthnow (1998, 9–10) described religious identity as shifting from a "spirituality of dwelling" to a "spirituality of seeking." He argues that an individual is no longer constrained by ascribed characteristics but rather, as "Sovereign Self," constructs his or her own personal religious identity by pulling together elements from various repertoires. Wade Clark Roof (1999) refers to this concept as the new "religious individualism." For Roof, "Individuals configure new spaces for making meaning and engage in a process of . . . authenticating their own affirmations" (1999, 166).

Jewish identities are no exception. They too have undertaken significant transformations. In the transition from premodern, traditional societies to post-Enlightenment, postmodern societies, Jewish cultural identities have shifted from an identity based on collectivism to an identity based on personalism and voluntarism (Cohen 1999; Elazar 1999). While in the past, Jewish identities were structured and regulated by the constraints of "normative community standards," in the modern period, cultural identities have come to be perceived as freely chosen and individually constructed (Bellah et al. 1985; Berger and Luckmann 1967). As such, many Jews in North America and elsewhere now feel free to appropriate only those aspects of Jewishness that they find personally meaningful (Cohen 1991; Cohen and Eisen 2000; Horowitz 1998).

North American Jews have thus come to view their Jewishness in a very different way than either their parents or they themselves did only two or three decades ago. Today's Jews—like members of other religious traditions—have turned inward in their search for meaning. This means that they have moved away from the organizations, institutions, and causes that used to anchor identity and shape behavior. As Michael Weil (2004) writes, "The so-called unaffiliated are doing and feeling things Jewish, but do it [and feel it] differently." They are turned off by the traditional modes of being Jewish, but rather than throwing in the towel they

have found meaningful Jewish replacements. Rather than con-
forming to a fixed Jewish identity given at birth, in the postmodern context each person now performs the labor of fashioning
his or her own self—pulling together elements from the various
Jewish repertoires available, sometimes combining these Jewish
elements with others drawn from the larger cultural milieu—
including non-Jewish religious or spiritual traditions. Many Jews
today still feel strongly Jewish—not because of any obligations to
the Jewish community or because of the historic "destiny" of the
Jewish people or out of a concern for Jewish continuity or survival, but simply because of what personal meaning being Jewish
may provide.

Alternative Sites of Jewish Culture and Association

Compared to their predecessors one or two generations ago,
North American Jews define themselves less and less by denominational boundaries (such as Orthodox, Conservative, Reform). In
some cases there is a deliberate blurring of denominational
boundaries. One of the fastest growing "denominations" in North
America today is aptly called "Just Jewish" (23 percent of American Jews according to the 2001 National Jewish Population Survey). The search for personal meaning does not lend itself well to
a strong affiliation to one of the highly structured ideological
movements of Judaism. Instead there is a growth in nondenominational and independent synagogues and other religious or spiritual groups and initiatives—thus the rise in nondenominational
Jewish day schools, of which the genesis and development of
DJDS is a case in point.

Part of this new meaning-based approach to Jewish identity is
the important realization that a person's experience of Jewishness
is a fluid rather than fixed aspect of their lives. Individuals often go
through "Jewish journeys" where Jewish identity evolves over the
life course, paralleling growth and personal development (Horowitz 2000). There is no end point, no arrival, no final answers.
These journeys can intensify with age, especially through the
agency of one's children or family. Decisions about ritual obser-

vance and involvement in Jewish institutions are made and made again, considered and reconsidered, year by year and even week by week. Personal meanings are sought for new as well as inherited observances. If these meanings are not found, the practices are modified or discarded. As our discussion has revealed, one's children's school is no exception. Parents are constantly reassessing how the school contributes to, among other things, the family's Jewish capital. Parents do not hesitate to withdraw their children and themselves from the school if they are not getting customer satisfaction from the product. By the same token, they are also prepared to make changes in their own lives if sufficiently engaged by meaningful enough experiences at the school. Parents' lives are thus open to being changed by and in relation to their children's school, unlikely as this may seem, given the limited ability of schools to effect change in the life chances of many children.

As Horowitz (2000) aptly points out, older understandings of Jewish identity asked the question "How Jewish are American Jews?"—making use of normative measurement criteria or operational definitions. Newer understandings of Jewish identity have provocatively modified the question to ask, "How are American Jews Jewish?"—thus shifting the enquiry from objective to subjective meanings of Jewishness.

Our work thus adds more evidence to an important discovery among social scientists who examine the construction of modern Jewish identity: Jewish adults are finding Jewish meaning in new and innovative ways, and in the process venerable institutions are being called upon to play new roles in Jewish society. Whereas older models in the study of Jewish identity see the enactment of Jewish religious rituals, such as synagogue service attendance, as the central definition of what it means to be Jewish in North America, newer perspectives point to a great variety of ways that Jews "do Jewish" today. Some of these ways include the embrace of Klezmer music or of the Yiddish language, involvement in political activism as it pertains to Israel, immersion in Jewish studies at the university, Israeli dancing at the local Jewish community centre, or participation in Jewish heritage travel or birthright Israel trips. Finding Jewish meaning through one's children's school is another instance of adults creating lived religion within an alternative Jewish site, surprising as this may seem given the absence of an explicit adult orientation within most elementary schools.

As indicated in an earlier chapter, there are other scholars who are exploring similar themes. Prell's (1989) study of a Los Angeles *havurah* group, Kliger's (1988) research into immigrant associations, Schwartz's (1988) work on "secular seders," and Grant et al.'s (2004) investigation of adult study groups all explore the search for individual experience in alternative Jewish settings. In all of these instances, "beyond the synagogue walls," as Davidman (2003) puts it, there are Jews who are not affiliated with conventional synagogues who take their Jewish identities quite seriously. As Jews in North America bring to the table less and less Jewish social and cultural capital, we suggest that these nontraditional or "alternative" ways of doing Jewish are likely to become more significant as gateways to Jewish association. As parents with few formal Jewish associations become increasingly prepared to spend more than ten thousand dollars a year on their children's Jewish schooling, the distinctions between high, moderate, and minimal Jewish affiliation are ever more confused. And with a narrowing of the differences between the sociological profile of those who do and do not send their children to day school, the culture-building potential of the day school as an "alternative" arena for adult Jewish identification becomes that much greater.

Lessons for Schools

What, then, ought to be the response of today's day-school educators to changed patterns of adult identification? What practical lessons can be learned from our account of DJDS parents and their children's school? What does our account imply for the future of day-school education?

Before addressing these larger questions, we spell out some more specific implications for schools as suggested by chapters 2–6. We provide a summation of each chapter's key findings and then suggest what these imply for practitioners.

Chapter 2: In chapter 2 we found that day-school choice is shaped by a mix of four factors: (1) parents' general ambivalence toward parochial Jewish schools, (2) their search for a quality education for their children, (3) their concern for their children's Jewish future, and (4) a factor until now overlooked in research on Jewish school choice, their search for an institution that can satisfy some of their own personal and social needs as Jewish adults.

This mix of concerns implies that when parents choose an elementary school for their child they are not just interested in whether the school is on the inside-track to the Ivy League. Literally and metaphorically, parents are looking for a school that *speaks to them.* Literally, speaking to them means that few parents want schools to release them fully of the burden of educating their children; most want to be consulted as partners in their children's education. Metaphorically, speaking to them means that parents want to readily understand what a school stands for and whether they can see themselves standing with it.

Marketing a Jewish elementary school is not, then, just about making sure parents know where past students graduated and with what grade average. Certainly it is important for schools to achieve and demonstrate educational quality, but it is critical also for them to help parents see whether they (as parents) "fit" the school, a concept we heard repeatedly in our interviews. This implies creating opportunities for prospective parents to meet current parents and not just to visit with the school's professionals. Parents want to see if members of the parent body are "their kind of folks." Schools' promotional literature should include plenty of quotes from parents, and not just the conventional kind where parents offer a paean to the quality education their children receive. These quotes should be about what parents do in the school and what they get out of the school. (On the DJDS Web site one of the most compelling items is a quote from a father who says, "We didn't just enroll our child in a day school, we joined a club.") Finally, if parents are to decide whether an institution fits them and their child, the school must promote itself in language that goes beyond generic promises of educational excellence. If parents are prepared to select a school rather than simply send their child to the most convenient local option, they seek clear and authentic alternatives, not cookie-cutter institutions whose mission statements are barely distinguishable from one another.

Chapter 3: In chapter 3 we found that parents become involved in schools for a range of purposes, some of which are not immediately obvious. Many of these involvements are concerned with facilitating the learning and development of their own child (the human-resource frame). At other times they are concerned with the well-being of the school as a whole (the structural frame) or with creating and directing school policy (the political frame). Less obviously, parents are also involved in the development and experience of shared Jewish meaning at school, culture-building work that has implications for the Jewish community as a whole (the symbolic frame).

The range of motivations behind parental participation in school life suggests that, contrary to the worst fears of many teachers, when parents do become deeply involved in school it is not necessarily (and even not likely to be) because they mistrust their children's teachers. If educators were alert to the variety of concerns that in fact underlie parents' interactions with them, it is probable that the relationships between parents and schools would be less charged.

We are familiar with a number of day schools that forbid parents from volunteering in their own children's classrooms. This policy, conceived to protect teachers from ceaseless parental scrutiny, disparages one of the primary pleasures of parent involvement—contact with one's own child—and overlooks some of the constructive ultimate purposes of such involvement. A parent's offer to help in the classroom need not be a stratagem for keeping an eye on the teacher. It may in fact reflect a concern to help the school operate more efficiently (the structural frame) or a desire to participate in meaningful aspects of school life (the symbolic frame). These goals, undeniably constructive within the development of school culture, become especially compelling when they provide parents with an opportunity to interact with their own child. They become much harder to realize when parents are required to volunteer only in other people's children's classrooms and are thereby denied a significant incentive for getting involved.

As we have written elsewhere, the existence of different ultimate purposes that underlie (frame) parental involvement indicates a need for both parents and teachers to better communicate their expectations and purposes to one another—that is, to calibrate the frames of school involvement (Pomson 2007). This means that parents must make their motives for involvement more explicit and that teachers must recognize the variety of legitimate purposes that bring parents into schools. Bridging the suspicion that separates parents and teachers might release profound cultural assets for schools already stretched thin in their attempt to fulfill their missions.

Chapter 4: In chapter 4 we saw that when viewed up close, the symbolic frame of school life (the ways parents find meaning within their children's school) parallels the sociological functions historically performed by the synagogue as *bet kenesset* (house of meeting), *bet midrash* (house of study), and *bet tephilah* (house of prayer). There is compelling evidence at DJDS of parents turning to and making use of the school as a site of social fellowship, education, and spiritual inspiration for themselves.

For many DJDS parents, their children's school has replaced the synagogue as their primary point of engagement with Jewish life. Such patterns are less widely repeated in other day-school settings where parents tend to maintain a much higher rate of synagogue membership. Nevertheless, it seems that the day school—an institution created to enable the *next* generation of adult Jews to participate knowledgably and responsibly in Jewish life—can and does provide a point of entry to meaningful Jewish engagement and learning for many in the present generation of adult Jews.

This is an outcome that few anticipated when day schools were first created in North America. It was previously assumed that families who were inclined to withdraw their children from the public school system would possess Jewish social and cultural resources to buttress the fortress of the Jewish day school. Today's day school parents are different. Many rely on their children's schools to provide the Jewish knowledge, inspiration, and community they don't possess at home. Some even seek that knowledge, inspiration, and community for themselves and not just for their children. Schools, however, are not generally staffed by professionals who are either inclined toward or adept at providing those services to adults.

Most day-school professionals took up their work because they enjoy working with children. They are stimulated by the company of young people and by the opportunity to help shape their young lives. Some educators, in fact, are uncomfortable when it comes to working with adults. The most competent of them can seem awkward on parent-teacher nights when they have to communicate with adults rather than with children. Schools must thus figure out who in their faculty will service the needs of parents and how they will go about doing this in ways that are not considered patronizing or prescriptive. As will be seen in a later section of this chapter, these are difficult questions that call for a reassessment of the day school's mission within contemporary Jewish society.

Chapter 5: In chapter 5 we saw that the school at home is a source for both Jewish social and cultural capital. Through the mediation of their children and at private, often deeply meaningful moments, parents acquire new Jewish social connections and new Jewish knowledge. Social and cultural capital is not simply deposited at home by children returning from school. Parents process, adapt, and ultimately syncretize capital with and within an already existing family culture.

It ought to be reassuring to Jewish educators that what children learn in school can have so much importance at home. Researchers have for years cautioned about the obstacles to transferring knowledge from one classroom to another, let alone from the school to sites outside the school doors. The fact that knowledge gained at school does make it home must surely be a positive finding. But educators also need to be aware that what children take home from school is not simply reproduced there. It is syncretized within family cultures in ways that are always idiosyncratic and often surprising. Furthermore, the families that are most engaged by the school and by what children bring home (those, we found, who came to the school with limited Jewish social and cultural capital) are the families who are likely to weave school and home together in the most unconventional ways. Teachers need to consider carefully how they react to these outcomes, for just as children take home what they learned at school, they also bring back to school the full range of practices and ideas that are constructed and reconstructed in their homes.

Chapter 6: Finally, the findings from chapter 6 emphasize that the problems and possibilities created by the changed relationships between parents and their children's schools are not confined to some freakish minority. They occur across North America in non-Orthodox or community schools and even in many Orthodox schools. They can also occur in schools of different size and age and in more than one cultural context. DJDS is undeniably the product of downtown Toronto culture, but the phenomena we saw so clearly there occur elsewhere, if less intensively, in a great variety of settings.

Between Educational Policy and Sociology

Sitting at the cusp of the two disciplines of education and sociology, the foregoing account can be concluded in two possible ways: first with a series of educational prescriptions derived from the implications gathered earlier, and second with a summative or synthetic sketch that draws together some of the sociological themes explored. We take up both options, starting first with what we suggest are appropriate programmatic responses to the phenomena we observed and finishing with a synthetic sociological representation of the day school, which we hope will provoke further debate about its role in contemporary Jewish society.

Some Educational Prescriptions

If, as our inquiry suggests, DJDS and other day schools have the potential to serve as important arenas for adult Jewish identification, even (if not, especially) for those with limited Jewish social and cultural capital, then the following must also occur.

SCHOOLS MUST TAKE INTO ACCOUNT THE PARTICULAR NEEDS OF ADULT CLIENTS.

At DJDS and at the other schools we studied, parents get involved and respond to their children's learning in order to live Jewishly, "to do Jewish," but rarely to study Judaism for its own sake. Their learning is a consequence rather than a cause of their involvement. They learn while doing or in order to do, and they learn most from peers rather than from an instructor. Generally they do not get involved in order to learn. (That's why so few turn up at adult education programs organized by the school.) This makes them quite different from that other group of somewhat older Jewish adults who have been much studied recently—those adult learners who sign up for learning programs, trips to Israel, and second bar mitzvahs (see, e.g., Grant et al. 2004; Schuster 2003).

If day schools are serious about engaging the Jewish social and cultural needs of parents, it is not more adult or parent education they should offer but rather a variation on the field of family education that has emerged in Jewish congregational schools since the 1980s, something that might be called "Jewish family experience." The difference between "family experience" and "family education" is much like the difference between camping and schooling. Camping can be an educational experience, but it is not an explicitly didactic one in the way school is. Parents, we believe, will only respond to a nondidactic approach to Jewish education where, as adults, they can have Jewish experiences (with their children and sometimes without them), where they can meet other Jews and simply enjoy one another's company, where they can do Jewish things and take responsibility for other Jews, and where in the process they will likely become Jewishly more knowledgeable and more engaged.

SCHOOLS AND COMMUNITIES MUST PLAN CAREFULLY
FOR THE DAY AFTER GRADUATION.

Although our research lacks a longitudinal dimension that tells us what happens to families once their children graduate day school, we expect that parents will have a different relationship with their children and with their children's Jewish education when their children move on to high school (Jewish or otherwise). We plan to return to DJDS in a few years' time in order to explore the longer term consequences of what we observed, but for the moment we suspect that if the connections that have sprung up around the school are to survive, they will need to be nurtured around additional foci. At this time, these connections, while meaningful as adult experiences, are ultimately contingent on the presence and inspiration of children. When children withdraw from the base of these connections, the surviving superstructure may be no more than a fragile web of memories and good intentions unless planfully sustained.

SCHOOLS MUST BUILD BRIDGES TO THE COMMUNITY BEYOND.

Day schools have provoked resentment among Jewish community leaders, especially among those who disapprove of the withdrawal of Jewish children from public education settings. Schools have been seen as diverting scarce resources to an indulged minority who are interested only in their own sectarian needs.

The schools we have studied do not tend to be enclaves for self-sufficient elites. (As we indicated earlier, DJDS families more resemble the Jewish families whose children do not attend day school than most of those who do.) But it is not yet known whether those parents who display leadership at DJDS, or simply are involved there, will also be inclined to participate in the life of the Jewish community beyond the school. We have noted on more than one occasion how parents were attracted to the school precisely because it was not compromised by or overburdened with the institutional baggage that makes more conventional settings so unappealing. Both school leaders and community leaders need to figure out how they can serve one another; otherwise what started out as an alternative and counter-cultural project for the (less than) moderately affiliated will remain just that, with little lasting benefit for the community.

Sociological Images: Between Neighborhood and Community

At various moments in this book we have taken up different metaphors to evoke the assorted qualities of life at DJDS for parents. Some of these metaphors were suggested by those we interviewed. Ruth Goldman, for example, talked of the school as "a bouquet of flowers," an image that captured the qualities of a community that came together not despite of but because of its diversity. Maytal Hillberg pictured the school as "a little island of Judaism in the city's downtown," emphasizing what people share when they join the school and what distinguishes them from the world outside. We reported how, at a meeting for new parents and their older buddies, one "old-timer" parent talked about the school as being like a summer camp in that it was a place where Judaism was fun and where people (young and old) were free to explore their own identities.

We suggested other metaphors to communicate important aspects of what we observed: the notion of the "school as shul," for example, was intended to convey the way the school has become a place of meeting, study, and spiritual inspiration for parents. The image of the school as a "thin place" we took from Celtic folklore to suggest how at DJDS—and perhaps schools in general—intimations of the ultimate lurk just below the surface of the mundane affairs of school life. Day schools, we found, provide the kind of spiritual inspiration than is often inaccessible within the scripted formality of synagogues.

As we draw together the threads of our discussion of the day school's role within a context of changing patterns of adult Jewish identification, we propose one final metaphor that conveys the sociological reality described in this book and that also suggests provocative policy implications if more schools are to cultivate the kinds of relationships and outcomes we observed.

It seems to us that in social and cultural terms the Jewish day school in relation to its parent body operates much as the Jewish street or neighborhood once did, at least during the first half of the twentieth century in major North American cities. In works of fiction (such as Bellow 1956; Roth 1934/1991; Yezierska 1920/1997), journalism (such as Cahan 1898), and sociology (e.g., Diner 2004; Moore 1987), young people or adult newcomers to Jewish neighborhoods are depicted as acquiring Jewish opinions, values, and language by virtue of their interaction with the unusual concentration of Jewish people and institutions in these spaces. Chance encounters and daily relationships with other Jewish people, access to diverse Jewish cultural and intellectual resources, and the experience of Jewish entertainment, literature, and conversation, all contributed to a process of Jewish socialization and acculturation that often lasted a lifetime no matter how far one strayed.

For parents there is much that happens in the classrooms, corridors, and committees of day schools that evokes these same acculturative processes. No doubt, at certain times of day, schools are quiet places, where the muffled noise of activity can be heard from behind closed classroom doors and where adults walk the corridors softly so as not to disturb the children within. At these times, although quietly inspiring for adults, there is no question that schools are, first and foremost, sites of learning for children. But then at other moments, school buildings erupt with energy, sound, and movement, as children spill into corridors and school yards. At these times parents can be submerged too. Particularly at the start and end of the day, adults coming into schools for all kinds of reasons brush pass and bump into friends or neighbors. They make arrangements and exchange information and gossip. And as on the street, in the school parking lot or lobby they make friends and learn norms, values, and language.

At other times of day, at moments rarely studied by sociologists of schooling, such as when the final school bell has rung, there are often only adults left in the building—janitorial staff restore order to the classrooms, teaching staff make preparations for the next day, and, sometimes until late at night, there are groups of parents in committee rooms and meeting spaces, immersed in school business. At these times, and in these rooms, the conduct of business is also an occasion, as on the street, for exchanging opinions, learning values, and making friends.

Finally, but more rarely, parents and children come together in schools for entertainment and inspiration. At these special moments, such as during festive seasons, it seems as though everyone in the neighborhood is present. There is a kind of heightened sense of possibility in the air fed by children rushing back and forth in costume and by the colorful appearance of specially decorated corridor walls. At such moments there is a palpable feeling of community and of shared interest, values, and purpose.

While there is a special sense of fellowship and inspiration at these special times, we resist employing the term *community* to depict the day-to-day experience of school for parents. The term has been overused in recent years in describing the work of schools, and the sense of social obligation it carries may be too burdensome for the sometimes-ephemeral relationships that are struck up among parents at school. For us, the idea of the day school as a kind of Jewish neighborhood better conveys the sense of shared space, of purposeful interaction, and of projects advanced, but where ultimate purposes are focused elsewhere—that is, not on the parents but on the children. Of course, this is an environment that can have a powerful socializing effect on those who experience it, but this environment, at least as far as we have seen, is rarely designed with a particular didactic purpose or agenda in relation to the adults who frequent it.

For some, that is as it should be. Schools are for children, and if parents benefit, that is all to the good, but that's not what school people are paid to attend to. Besides, even seen in these terms, as neighborhood rather than community, a heavy burden rests on those who run schools. Neighborhoods need maintenance if they are to function productively and are not quickly to decay. Their merits need to be advertised if people are to come visit, live, or work. There is much to be done if the day school is to function well as an alternative Jewish neighborhood for parents.

If, however, one is of the opinion that schools are not only for children and that neighborhoods, for all their utility, do not compare in quality of life or significance to communities, then the time has come to rethink the practices of the Jewish day school. Conceived originally as a vehicle for the intensive socialization and education of Jewish children, the day school will need to function differently if it is to be a site of community for adults. In this book we have provided intimations of what that might involve. We have discussed how faculty and families can create an environment that provides families with a sense of being part of a larger whole, both culturally and socially. But we have also seen that this environment has not in the main been planfully cultivated to produce such an effect. If schools seek purposefully to produce these outcomes, they need to think carefully about how parents, focused first on the needs of their children, will come to experience and find meaning from their contact with and involvement at school. Our sense is that at DJDS they have made a start toward just such a community, if at times by accident rather than by design; for other parents and other schools the journey has yet to begin.

References

Acker, S. 1999. *The realities of teachers' work: Never a dull moment.* New York: Cassell.

Ackerman, W. 1969. Jewish education for what? In *American Jewish Yearbook,* 3–36. Philadelphia: Jewish Publication Society.

———. 1989. Strangers to tradition: Idea and constraint in American Jewish education. In *Jewish education worldwide: Cross-cultural perspectives,* ed. H. S. Himmelfarb and S. DellaPergolla, 71–116. Lanham, MD: University Press of America.

Ayers, W. 2000. Simple justice: Thinking about teaching and learning, enquiry and the fight for small schools. In *A simple justice: The challenge of small schools,* ed. W. Ayers, M. Klonsky, and G. Lyon, 1–8. New York: Teachers College Press.

Barack Fishman, S. 1995. *Jewish education and Jewish identity among contemporary American Jews: Suggestions from current research.* Boston: Bureau of Jewish Education, Centre for Educational Research and Evaluation.

Bauch, P. 1989. Linking parents' reasons for choice or involvement in inner-city Catholic high schools. *International Journal of Education* 15:311–22.

Beck, P. 2002. *Jewish preschools as gateways to Jewish life: A survey of Jewish preschool parents in three cities.* Baltimore: Jewish Early Childhood Education Partnership.

Beinart, P. 1999. October: The rise of the Jewish school. *Atlantic Monthly,* 21–23.

Bellah, R. N., R. Madsen, W. A. Sullivan, A. Swidler, and S. M. Tipton. 1985. *Habits of the heart: Individualism and commitment in American life.* Berkeley: University of California Press.

Bellow, S. 1956. *The victim.* New York: Viking.

Berger, P. 1967. *The sacred canopy.* Garden City, NY: Anchor.

Berger, P. L., and T. Luckmann. 1967. *The social construction of reality: A treatise in the sociology of knowledge.* Garden City, NY: Doubleday.

Bolman, L. G., and T. E. Deal. 2003. *Reframing organizations: Artistry, choice and leadership* (3rd ed.). San Francisco: Jossey-Bass.

Bourdieu, P. 1986. The forms of capital. Trans. R. Nice. In *Handbook of theory and research for the sociology of education*, ed. J. C. Richardson, 241–58. New York: Greenwood Press.

Britzman, D. 1991. *Practice makes practice: A critical study of learning to teach.* Albany: State University of New York Press.

Brodbar-Nemzer, J., S. M. Cohen, A. Reitzes, C. Shahar, and G. Tobin. 1993. An overview of the Canadian Jewish community. In *The Jews in Canada*, ed. R. J. Brym, W. Shaffir, and M. Weinfeld, 39–72. Toronto: Oxford University Press.

Bryk, A., V. Lee, and P. B. Holland. 1993. *Catholic schools and the common good.* Cambridge, MA: Harvard University Press.

Bullivant, B. 1983. Transmission of tradition in an Orthodox day school: An ethnographic case study. *Studies in Jewish Education* 1:39–72.

Cahan, A. 1898. The Russian Jew in America. *Atlantic Monthly*, July, 130–33.

Central Advisory Council for Education. 1967. *Children and their primary schools.* London: Her Majesty's Stationery Office.

Cohen, S. M. 1991. *Content or Continuity? Alternative Bases for Commitment.* New York: American Jewish Committee.

———. 1995. The impact of varieties of Jewish education upon Jewish identity: An intergenerational perspective. *Contemporary Jewry* 16:68–96.

———. 1999. Introduction. In *National Variations in Jewish Identity: Implications for Jewish Education*, ed. Steven M. Cohen and Gabriel Horencyzk, 1–17. Albany: State University of New York Press.

Cohen, S., and A. Eisen. 2000. *The Jew within: Self, family, and community in America.* Bloomington: Indiana University Press.

Cohen, S., and S. Kelner. 2007. Why Jewish parents send their children to Jewish day schools. In *Family matters: Jewish education in an age of choice*, ed. Jack Wertheimer, 80–100. Hanover, NH: University Press of New England.

Coleman, J. 1990. *Foundations of social theory.* Cambridge, MA: Belknap Press.

———. 1994. Family involvement in education. In *Parents, their children, and schools*, ed. B. Schneider and J. Coleman, 23–37. Boulder, CO: Westview Press.

Coleman, J., E. Campbell, C. Hobson, J. McPartland, A. Mood, F. D. Weinfeld, and R. York. 1966. *Equality of educational opportunity.* Washington, DC: Department of Health, Education, and Welfare.

Coleman, J., and T. Hoffer. 1987. *Public and private high schools: The impact of communities.* New York: Basic Books.

Crozier, G. 2000. *Parents and schools: Partners or protagonists.* Stoke-on-Trent, UK: Trentham Books.

Cutler, W. 2000. *Parents and schools: The 150-Year struggle for control in American education.* Chicago: University of Chicago Press.

DAF [Jewish Day School Advocacy Forum]. 2006. www.jdaf.net/story.html (accessed September 5, 2006).

Danielewicz, J. 2001. *Teaching selves: Identity, pedagogy, and teacher education.* Albany: State University of New York Press.

Davidman, L. 2003. Beyond the synagogue walls. In *Handbook of the sociology of religion,* ed. M. Dillon, 260–75. Cambridge: Cambridge University Press.

Davie, G. 1994. *Religion in Britain since 1945: Believing without belonging.* Oxford: Blackwell.

Della Pergola, S., and U. O. Schmelz. 1989. Demography and Jewish education in the Diaspora: Trends in Jewish school-age population and school enrollment. In *Jewish education worldwide: Cross-cultural perspectives,* ed. H. S. Himmelfarb and S. Della Pergola, 43–68. Lanham, MD: University Press of America.

Delpit, L. 1993. *Other people's children: Cultural conflict in the classroom.* New York: New Press.

Dewey, J. 1902/1990. *The school and society: The child and the curriculum* (Rev. ed.). Chicago: University of Chicago Press.

Diamond, E. 2000. *And I will dwell in their midst: Orthodox Jews in suburbia.* Chapel Hill: University of North Carolina Press.

Diner, H. R. 2004. *The Jews of the United States, 1654 to 2000.* Berkeley: University of California Press.

DiQuinzio, P. 1999. *The impossibility of motherhood: Feminism, individualism and the problem of motherhood.* London: Routledge.

Drachler, N., ed. 1996. *A bibliography of Jewish education in the United States.* Detroit: Wayne State University Press.

Driscoll, M. E. 1995. Thinking like a fish: The implications of the image of school community for connections between parents and school. In *Transforming schools,* ed. P. Cookson Jr. and B. Schneider, 209–36. New York: Garland.

Elazar, D. J. 1999. Jewish religious, ethnic, and national identities: Convergences and conflicts. In *National variations in Jewish identity: Implications for Jewish education,* ed. S. M. Cohen and G. Horencyzk, 35–52. Albany: State University of New York Press.

Epstein, J. L. 1994. Theory to practice: School and family partnerships lead to school improvement and student success. In *Parents, their children, and schools*, ed. B. Schneider and J. Coleman, 40–52. Boulder, CO: Westview Press.

Epstein, J. L., and M. G. Sanders. 2000. Connecting home, school and community. In *Handbook of the sociology of education*, ed. M. T. Hallinan, 285–306. New York: Kluwer.

Fine, M. 1993. [Ap]parent involvement: Reflections on parents, power, and urban public schools. *Teachers College Record* 94 (4): 682–729.

Flyvbjerg, B. 2006. Five misunderstandings about case study research. *Qualitative Inquiry* 12 (2): 219–45.

Furman, F. K.. 1987. *Beyond Yiddishkeit: The struggle for Jewish identity in a Reform synagogue*. Albany: State University of New York Press.

Gamoran, A., W. G. Secada, and C. A. Marrett. 2000. The organizational context of teaching and learning: Changing theoretical perspectives. In *Handbook of sociology of education*, ed. M. T. Hallinan, 37–63. New York: Kluwer Academic.

Gibbs, N. 2005 (February 21). What teachers hate about parents. *Time*, 165, 40–49.

Goldring, E., and R. Shapira. 1993. Choice, empowerment and involvement: What satisfies parents? *Educational Evaluation and Policy Analysis* 15 (4): 396–409.

Goodkind, E. R. 1994. Preface. In *The Jewish family and Jewish continuity*, ed. S. Bayme and G. Rosen, vii–x. Hoboken, NJ: KTAV Publishing House.

Grant, L. D. 2001. The role of mentoring in enhancing experience of a congregational Israel trip. *Journal of Jewish Education* 67 (1/2): 46–60.

Grant, L. D., D. Tickton-Schuster, M. Woocher, and S. M. Cohen. 2004. *A journey of heart and mind: Transformative Jewish learning in adulthood*. New York: JTS Press.

Hall, D., ed. 1997. *Lived religion in America*. Princeton, NJ: Princeton University Press.

Hall, S. 1997. The work of representation. In *Representation: Cultural representations and signifying practices*, ed. S. Hall, 13–74. London: Sage/Open University.

Hargreaves, A. 1999. Professional and parents: A social movement for educational change. Invited address to the Times Educational Supplement Leadership Seminar, University of Keele, April 27. www.keele.ac.uk/depts/ed/kisnet/interviews/hargreaves.htm (accessed December 19, 2005).

Heilman, S. 1976. *Synagogue life: A study in symbolic interaction.* Chicago: University of Chicago Press.

———. 1984. *Inside the Jewish school: A study of the cultural setting for Jewish education.* New York: American Jewish Committee.

Henry, M. 1993. *School cultures: Universes of meaning in private schools.* Norwood, NJ: Ablex.

Hoover-Dempsey, K. V., and H. M. Sandler. 1997. Why do parents become involved in their children's education? *Review of Educational Research* 67 (1): 3–42.

Horowitz, B. 1998. Connections and journeys: Studying identities among American Jews. *Contemporary Jewry* 19:63–94.

———. 2000. *Connections and journeys: Assessing critical opportunities for enhancing Jewish identity.* New York: UJA-Federation of Jewish Philanthropies for New York.

Hughes, M., F. Wikeley, and T. Nash. 1994. *Parents and their children's schools.* Oxford: Blackwell.

James, W. 1902/2002. *Varieties of religious experience: A study in human nature.* New York: Routledge.

Jenkins, R. 1996. *Social identity.* London: Routledge.

Kapel, D. 1972. Parental views of a Jewish day school. *Jewish Education* 41 (3): 28–38.

Kaplowitz, T. 2002. Community building: A new role for the Jewish school. *Journal of Jewish Education* 68 (3): 29–48.

Kaufman, D. 1999. *Shul with a pool: The "synagogue-center" in American Jewish history.* Hanover, NH: University Press of New England.

Kelman, S. L. 1979. Motivation and goals: Why parents send their children to non-Orthodox day schools. *Jewish Education* 47 (1): 44–48.

———. 1984. Why parents send their children to non-Orthodox Jewish day schools: A study of motivations and goals. *Studies in Jewish Education* 2:289–98.

Keyes, C. 2005. Parent-teacher partnerships, challenging but essential. *Teachers College Record,* May 16, 2005. www.tcrecord.org (accessed July 17, 2006).

Kirschenblatt-Gimblett, B. (n.d.). Learning from ethnography: Reflections on the nature and efficacy of youth tours to Israel. In *Studies in Jewish identity and youth culture,* ed. B. Chazan, 269–331. New York: Andrea and Charles Bronfman Philanthropies.

Kliger, H. 1988. A home away from home: Participation in immigrant associations in America. In *Persistence and flexibility: Anthropological perspectives on the American Jewish experience,* ed. W. Zenner, 139–64. Albany: State University of New York Press.

Kovács, E., and J. Vajda. 2002. Interchanged identities: The role of a Jewish school in a mixed marriage. *History of the Family* 7:239–57.

Kugelmass, J. 1986. *The miracle of Intervale Avenue: The story of a Jewish congregation in the South Bronx.* New York: Schocken.

Lareau, A. 2000. *Home advantage: Social class and parental intervention in elementary education.* Lanham, MD: Rowman and Littlefield.

Lawrence-Lightfoot, S. 1978. *Worlds apart: Relationships between families and schools.* New York: Basic Books.

Levine, L. I. 1987. The Second Temple Synagogue: The formative years. In *The synagogue in late antiquity,* ed. L. I. Levine, 7–31. Philadelphia: American Schools of Oriental Research.

Lewis, S. 1999. *Reinventing ourselves after motherhood: How former career women refocus their personal and professional lives after the birth of a child.* Lincolnwood, IL: Contemporary.

Lipset, S. M. 1994. *The power of Jewish education.* Los Angeles: Susan and David Wilstein Institute of Jewish Policy Studies.

Lortie, D. C. 1975. *Schoolteacher: A sociological study.* Chicago: University of Chicago Press.

Mattingly, D. J., R. Prislin, T. L. McKenzie, J. L. Rodrigues, and B. Kayzar. 2002. Evaluating evaluations: The case of parent involvement programs. *Review of Educational Research* 72 (4): 549–76.

McLaren, P. 1986. *Schooling as ritual performance: Towards a political economy of educational symbols and gestures.* London: Routledge and Kegan Paul.

McNeal, R. B. 1999. Parental involvement as social capital: Differential effectiveness on science achievement, truancy and dropping out. *Social Forces* 78 (1): 117–44.

Merz, C., and G. Furman. 1997. *Community and schools: Promise and paradox.* New York: Teachers College Press.

Moore, D. Dash. 1987. The construction of community: Jewish migration and ethnicity in the United States. In *The Jews of North America,* ed. Moses Rischin, 105–17. Detroit: Wayne State University Press.

Munn, P., ed. 1993. *Parents and schools: Customers, managers or partners.* London: Routledge.

Myerhoff, B. 1979. *Number our days.* New York: E. P. Dutton.

Nagel, J. 1994. Constructing ethnicity: Creating and recreating ethnic identity and culture. *Social Problems* 41 (1): 152–76.

Orsi, R. 1999. *Gods of the city: Religion and the American urban landscape.* Bloomington: Indiana University Press.

Ostrom, V., and E. Ostrom. 1971. Public choice: A different approach to the study of public administration. *Public Administration Review* 31:203–16.

Otto, R. 1965. *The idea of the holy: An inquiry into the nonrational factor in the idea of the divine and its relation to the rational.* New York: Oxford University Press.

Peshkin, A. 2001. *Permissible advantage? The moral consequences of elite schooling.* Mahwah, NJ: Lawrence Erlbaum Associates.

Pomson, A. 2004. Day School parents and their children's schools. *Contemporary Jewry.* 24:104–23.

———. 2007. Schools for parents? What parents want and what they get from their children's Jewish day schools. In *Family matters: Jewish education in an age of choice,* ed. J. Wertheimer, 101–42. Hanover, NH: University Press of New England.

———. In press. "Dorks in yarmulkes": An ethnographic inquiry into the surprised embrace of parochial day schools by liberal American Jews. In *Cultural education, cultural sustainability,* ed. Z. Beckerman and E. Kopelowitz. London: Routledge.

Prell, R.-E. 1989. *Prayer and community: The Havurah in American Judaism.* Detroit: Wayne State University Press.

———. 2007. Jewish families and education: How children's uniqueness and parental choice will shape American Judaism in the twenty-first century. In *Family matters: Jewish education in an age of choice,* ed. J. Wertheimer, 3–33. Hanover, NH: University Press of New England.

Putnam, R. D. 2000. *Bowling Alone: The collapse and revival of American community.* New York: Simon and Schuster.

Rawidowicz, S. 1986. *Israel: The ever-dying people and other essays.* Cranbury, NJ: Associated University Presses.

Reimer, J. 1997. *Succeeding at Jewish education: How one synagogue made it work.* Philadelphia: Jewish Publication Society.

Roof, W. Clark. 1999. *Spiritual Marketplace: Baby Boomers and the Remaking of American Religion.* Princeton, NJ: Princeton University Press.

———. 2003. Religion and spirituality: Toward an integrated analysis. In *Handbook of the sociology of religion,* ed. Michelle Dillon, 137–48. Cambridge: Cambridge University Press.

Roth, H. 1934/1991. *Call it sleep.* New York: Farrar, Straus & Giroux.

Sarason, S. B. 1990. *The predictable failure of educational reform: Can we change course before it's too late?* San Francisco: Jossey Bass

———. 1996. Revisiting *"The culture of the school and the problem of change."* New York: Teachers College Press.

Sarna, J. 1998. American Jewish education in historical perspective. *Journal of Jewish Education* 64 (1–2): 8–21.

Schick, M. 2005. *A census of Jewish day schools in the United States, 2003–2004.* New York: Avi Chai Foundation.

Schiff, A. 1974. Jewish day schools in the United States. *Encyclopedia Judaica Year Book.* Jerusalem: Keter.

Schnoor, R. F. 2006. Being gay and Jewish: Negotiating intersecting identities. *Sociology of Religion* 67 (1): 43–60.

Schoenfeld, S. 1990. Some aspects of the social significance of Bar-Bat Mitzvah celebrations. In *Essays in the social scientific study of Judaism and Jewish society,* Vol. 1, ed. Simcha Fishbane, 277–304. Montreal: Concordia University, Department of Religion.

Schuster, D. Tickton. 2003. *Jewish lives, Jewish learning: Adult Jewish learning in theory and practice.* New York: UAHC Press.

Schwartz, A. 1988. The secular seder: Continuity and change among left wing Jews. In *Between two worlds: Ethnographic essays on American Jewry,* ed. J. Kugelmas, 105–27. Ithaca, NY: Cornell University Press.

Sergiovanni, T. 2000. *The lifeworld of leadership: Creating culture, community, and personal meaning in our schools.* San Francisco: Jossey-Bass.

Shaffir, W., and M. Weinfeld. 1981. Canada and the Jews: An introduction. In *The Canadian Jewish mosaic,* ed. M. Weinfeld, W. Shaffir, and I. Cotler, 7–20. Toronto: John Wiley and Sons.

Shapiro, S. 1996. A parent's dilemma: Public vs. Jewish education. *Tikkun Magazine* 17 (4): 13–16.

Shields, C. 2000. Learning from difference: Considerations for schools as communities. *Curriculum Inquiry* 30 (3): 275–94.

Shrager, H. 2002, May 21. More Jewish day schools open as parents reconsider values. *Wall Street Journal.* http://groups.yahoo.com/group/SepSchool/message/5277?source=1 (accessed December 7, 2003).

Sklare, M. [1955] 1972. *Conservative Judaism: An American religious movement.* New York: Schocken.

Smrekar, C. 1996. *The impact of school choice and community: In the interest of families and schools.* New York: Teachers College Press.

Smrekar, C., and E. Goldring. 1999. *School choice in urban America: Magnet schools and the pursuit of equity.* New York: Teachers College Press.

Spector, M., and J. I. Kitsuse. 1987. *Constructing social problems.* New York: Aldine de Gruyter.

Stake, R. E. 1995. *The art of case study research.* Thousand Oaks, CA: Sage.

Tetlock, P. E., and A. Belkin, eds. 1996. *Counterfactual thought experiments in world politics: Logical, methodological, and psychological perspectives.* Princeton, NJ: Princeton University Press.

Tierney, W. G., and P. Dilley. 2002. Interviewing in education. In *Handbook of interview research: Context and method,* ed. J. F. Gubrium and J. A. Holstein, 453–71. Thousand Oaks, CA: Sage.

Tönnies, F. 1963. *Community and society (Gemeinschaft und Gesellschaft).* New York: Harper.

Turner, V. 1974. *Dramas, fields, and metaphors: Symbolic actions in human society.* Ithaca, NY: Cornell University Press.

———. 1982. *From ritual to theatre: The human seriousness of play.* New York: Performing Arts Journal.

Tyack, D., and W. Tobin. 1993. The "grammar" of schooling: Why has it been so hard to change? *American Educational Research Journal* 31 (3): 453–79.

Tye, B. B. 2000. *Hard truths: Uncovering the deep structure of schooling.* New York: Teachers College Press.

Van Mannen, J. 1988. *Tales of the field: On writing ethnography.* Chicago: University of Chicago Press.

Wall, S. 1995. *Parents of pre-schoolers: Their Jewish identity and its implications for Jewish education.* Unpublished PhD diss., Jewish Theological Seminary of America, New York.

Waller, W. 1935/1960. *The sociology of teaching.* New York: Russell and Russell.

Waters, M. C. 1990, *Ethnic options: Choosing identities in America.* Berkeley: University of California Press.

Webb, R., and G. Vulliamy. 1993. A deluge of directives: Conflict between collegiality and managerialism in the post ERA primary school. *British Education Research Journal* 22 (4): 441–58.

Weil, M. 2004. Rethinking unaffiliated Jews. *Jerusalem Post.* On-line edition. March 8. www.highbeam.com/doc/IPI-91989645.html (accessed on August 24, 2006).

Wertheimer, J. 1999. Jewish education in the United States: Recent trends and issues. In *America Jewish Yearbook, 99,* ed. D. Singer, 3–118. New York: American Jewish Committee.

———. 2005. The American synagogue: Recent trends and issues. *American Jewish Year Book, 105,* 3–83. New York: American Jewish Committee.

Wuthnow, R. 1998. *After heaven: Spirituality in America since the 1950s.* Berkeley: University of California Press.

Yezierska, A. 1920/1997. *Hungry hearts.* New York: Penguin.

Zeldin, M. 1988. *Cultural dissonance in Jewish education: The case of reform day schools.* Los Angeles: Hebrew Union College, Jewish Institute of Religion.

Index

Jewish day schools: in American suburbia, 21–22; attended by nearly
one-fourth of Jewish school-age children, 11; development of since
World War II, 10–11; dual curriculum of Jewish or Hebrew studies and
general studies, 32; important role
in personal and religious lives of parents, especially those with limited
Jewish social and cultural capital,
147–48; nondenominational, 154;
operate as the Jewish neighborhood
once did, 164–67; proportion of total
attendees at non-Orthodox schools,
11; role of in lives of some Jewish
adults, 3; size of, and parental
involvement, 135–36; special occasions convened for family members
of students, 83. *See also* school-
choice process
"Jewish family experience," 162
Jewish heritage travel, 155
Jewish identity: changing patterns of,
152–54; fluidity of, 111; new meaning-based approach to, 154–56; shift
from collectivism to personalism
and volunteerism, 153; shift from
objective to subjective meanings of
Jewishness, 155
"Jewish journeys," 154
Jewish schooling: alternative vision of
education from that provided by
public school system, 4; ethnographies of, 3; importance of in lives of
Jewish parents, 3; lessons from sociology for, 151–67; separation of
study from adult Jewish lives, 2. *See
also* Downtown Jewish Day School
(DJDS); Jewish day schools
Jewish studies, 155
Jews, North American: blurring of
denominational boundaries, 154;
inward search for meaning, 153–54;
view Jewishness in different way
from parents, 153
The Jew Within (Cohen and Eisen),
7–8
"Just Jewish," 154

Kaplan, Mordechai, 90
kashrut, 30
Kelner, Shaul, 57–58
Kiddush, 144
kippah, 144
Klezmer music, 155
kol nidre night, 106
Kovács, E., 3

large schools, can engender intense
and meaningful social interaction,
136
Lawrence-Lightfoot, Sara, 1
Leo Baeck Academy (pseud.), 15, 22,
32, 134, 136, 138–39, 145–46,
149–50
Levine, Lee I., 90
liberal Jews, drift toward parochial
schools, 37
liminal moments, 104; and blurring of
boundaries, 139
lived religion, 6; inward turn of, 133

magnet schools, 2
"Ma'oz Tzur," 106
Mattingly, D. J., 66
Merz, C., 60, 92
methodologies, 13–15
Miles Nidal Jewish Community Cen-
ter, 17–18
Montreal, 20

National Jewish Population Survey, 8
nondenominational Jewish day
schools, 154
nondenominational synagogues, 154
non-Orthodox day schools, 11, 32,
143, 161

Orthodox schools, and parents with
limited Jewish social and cultural
capital, 143

parashat hashavuah, 114
parental involvement in schools:
human-resource frame, 70–74; not
exclusively about quality of children's learning, 67; political frame,